The
Three R's

by Ruth Beechick

includes:
A Home Start in Reading
A Strong Start in Language
An Easy Start in Arithmetic

MO
MEI

Fenton, M.

Printed in the United States of America.

ISBN10: 0-88062-074-9
ISBN13: 978-0-88062-074-1

A Home Start in *READING*

Reading

Contents

Should you start reading as early as possible or delay until later? How do you know the right time for your child? What teaching can you do while waiting?

This is how to start easy in phonics, and how to make it fun.

Accomplish this crucial step and all the rest will be a downhill ride.

Here, at last, is the main part that people think is teaching reading. It includes directions for phonics and essential sight words, as well as writing and spelling that should happen during this step.

This is a necessary but often neglected step. Allow time for lots of easy reading instead of pushing relentlessly forward.

Introduction

Congratulations on your decision to teach your child at home. Home is the best of all possible environments for learning. These five steps to reading are for you if you intend to be your child's main teacher or if you wish to supplement the teaching he or she gets at school.

As you read this parent guide, you will find that the simple steps to reading remove the mystique that too often surrounds the subject. There is no real mystery about reading; it is only common sense for people like you, who read regularly and who buy books on how to teach their children. Learn the five steps, know where you are headed, and confidence will be yours.

This is one of the easiest guides to reading instruction that you will ever find. Extraneous theories and arguments about reading have been left out. Impractical, ivory-tower ideas are not here either. What you will find is a straight path through the reading maze, a path that has been traveled by hundreds of children that the author has led to a life of reading.

When can you start? Probably as soon as you familiarize yourself with the five steps. If your child is very young—say, anywhere from birth to four years old—you can start with Step 1 and move in the next few years through the rest of the steps. If your child is kindergarten or primary age you may plunge in at any step that seems to fit the child's needs. And if your child is older yet, but does not have a good start in reading, dip into these steps at various points. Give him anything he has missed or hasn't yet mastered.

How long can you use this guide? In grade level terms, the guide takes you through early reading, up to about fourth grade, the level where children can use their reading skills to learn history or science or any other subject found in books. In terms of age, the time varies widely. More on this in the steps themselves.

What curriculum or books do you need? This homespun, natural system of reading does not require expensive teaching materials. Actually, all you need are this guide and easy books that are available around your home and local libraries. A good argument for using homemade flashcards is that you won't be using them long, anyway. When you individualize for your child, you (or the child) make flashcards for something he needs to learn. Hopefully, in a few days, or at most a few weeks, he learns them and you move on to new lessons. You don't feel obliged to do more in order to "get your money's worth" out of a set of commercial cards. The same can be said for workbooks. Once the money is spent, there is a temptation to make the child work every line of every page whether he needs it or not. Parents then find themselves teaching a book or a course instead of teaching the child. But such materials are not precluded when you use this guide. You and your child may enjoy using them and may want them at various times, and you will find that practically any such materials easily fit into the steps described herein.

This guide is arranged with the five steps of reading described in the next five sections. In each section you get an explanation and overview of the step itself. In steps 2 through 5 you get basic teaching methods and a list of games and activities for adding occasional variety to the basics. In the latter steps you also get guidelines for teaching writing and spelling, as these skills must grow along with reading.

Before embarking on the steps, we pause for a word of caution. When any learning or developmental process is laid out in steps, the typical American reaction is to try to move children through the steps earlier and faster. Our ambitious, achievement-

Reading

oriented culture seems to demand this. If you have that common American characteristic, this caution is not to say you should change your values and desire less than the best for your child. But it is to remind you that there are other considerations besides moving up the steps. For one, there is the principle of optimum timing which will be explained later. For another, there is quality. The steps undergird a lifetime of reading and learning. So build the foundation by thoroughness and mastery, not just speed. And a third consideration is enjoyment. Too much pressure on a child can cause a dislike of reading and of books. The very goal you want the most can be lost. So move ahead at your child's own timing.

And now, on with the five steps for teaching your child to read.

STEP 1: Prereading

This step begins in babyhood with all the things you've heard about loving the child and letting him grow up confident and with a good measure of self-esteem. But let's assume that most of you reading this guide have already passed that time in your child's life.

If you are reading this guide, you probably are wondering when and how to begin teaching "reading." First, let's take up the question of when. That's very important. There has been much talk about it in recent years, and no doubt you can find among your friends both "early starters" and "late starters." The early starters have read books about how to teach their baby to read. They have labels on furniture, appliances, and doors all over the house. Their baby plays with word cards every day. The late starters are more relaxed. They read books too—the "late is better" variety. They read to their children. They teach them to cook and garden and help fix the car. And they won't be upset if a child doesn't show a desire to read until age eight or so.

Which of your friends are right? This guide will generally take you somewhere between those two extremes as it helps you individualize for your own child. In walking between the extremes, we probably lean more toward "late" than "early," not because there is anything especially wrong with the early systems, but because we have seen more damage done to the early children. It usually is not the baby who shows any readiness or eagerness to learn to read early, but it is too often an over-anxious mother pushing for it.

Occasionally in a family, older children will play school with a younger sibling and teach the child to read. In one family, the children sprawled around a newspaper each night and taught the youngest the letters and sounds in headlines. It was similar to playing with a doll, only this one was live, and particularly bright. She learned to read before age three and came to no harm because of it. Some mothers may enjoy playing with their "dolls" in this way and the children will not be harmed. Unfortunately, other mothers are feeding their own egos when they do this. Wanting their children to outdo other children, they pressure, and damage both the child's personality and the relationship between child and mother.

It is true that some children can learn to read remarkably early. But the fact that they *can* does not necessarily mean they *should*. *Should* is another question. One school district set up an experiment to help decide this question. Some kindergartners in the district received extensive instruction in reading. Others spent the same amount of time learning science. They melted ice. They observed thermometers in hot and cold places. They played with magnets, grew plants, learned about animal life, and so on. Books and pictures were available for these children if they wanted them, but no formal lessons in reading were held.

And what did the school district learn? By third grade the "science" children were far ahead of the "reading" children in their reading scores. The reason? Their vocabularies and thinking skills were more advanced. They could read on more topics and understand higher level materials. The "reading" children, by starting earlier, used up a lot of learning time on the skills of reading, while the "science" children spent the time learning real stuff. And when they did begin reading, they were older and knew more and learned in a fraction of the time that the others took.

This research and others like it are compelling. They drive home the fact that each child has only a limited amount of time in his early years. That time can be squandered in trying to teach reading before the "optimum" time for it. Or it can be used wisely in teaching "real stuff" that the child is ready for. If you are the teacher, the choice is yours.

The real stuff your child learns does not have to be only science. Science is a natural because children are curious about the world around them, and you can capitalize on that curiosity. But you can teach also about music, art, literature, money, work, safety, God, people, and everything else you and your child are interested in.

All such teaching is "prereading" instruction. It is getting ready for reading. Everything your child learns increases his vocabulary and develops his thinking skills. Now, you have been doing this for your child all along. How did he learn words so far? How did he learn the grammar necessary to form sentences? How did he learn to tell the chocolate milk carton from the white milk carton? The science research described above seems to be telling you to keep up that kind of informal teaching a little longer than most people would advise you to. The American attitude that "earlier is better" will die hard, in spite of research evidence to the contrary.

Prereading instruction, then, is wider than the whole world. Teach about the cooking and cleaning going on in your kitchen. Teach good eating habits, nutrition, care of teeth. And teach about the stars and the God who made them. Solve problems. How can we arrange the sleeping when Grandma comes to visit? How can we keep baby brother from eating the crayons? Read aloud to your child. Teach nursery rhymes. Ask questions and let the child ask you questions.

Some readers will say, "I've done all that. Now when do I start actual reading instruction?"

If you are in tune with your child, it is quite easy to tell when. Children have different ways of letting you know. Some begin asking about words and letters. Some learn favorite books by heart and sit reading them.

Put out trial balloons. Teach the child to write or pronounce one or more sounds. Is he interested in learning them? Or does he resist?

Your observations of the child and your trial balloons will tell you when to start. And the same skills will tell you all along the path just how fast to move.

Read the next step carefully. It likely is different from first reading steps that you have heard of elsewhere.

STEP 2: Beginning

Did you ever stop to think that you don't need to know the names of letters in order to read? That's right. To read *cat* or *dog*, you must know the sound of each letter but you do not need to know its name.

With a grasp of that principle, you have a shortcut to your child's reading. Do not burden her at the beginning with learning the names of twenty-six letters. Start by teaching the forms of the letters and their sounds. Begin with the child's own name and other high interest words. Later, for thoroughness, you can use a set of cards or a chart or list.

Let's say, for instance, that your child's name is Jenny. Print it with the *J* capitalized and the other letters in lower case. Say, "This says 'Jenny.'" Let the child look, trace with her fingers or a crayon, or make a copy, according to her ability. If this is the first time, you may guide her finger to trace the *J* only.

Take a shortcut with writing, too. Don't burden the child at the beginning with lines. Don't force her to decide how high to make each letter, how to make it sit on a line, when to go below the line, and so forth. Let her concentrate only on the form of the letter. Use unlined paper. Lines can come later when she has control of the forms.

Back to the word *Jenny*: trace the *J* make the sound /j/, and say "Jenny." (In this guide sounds are given between slashes and letters are given in italics.) After she recognizes her name and can print it, you can branch outward from that knowledge. Print *Jelly*. "J-jelly." Print *Jet*. "J-jet." Then print jelly and jet with lower case j's. Move on to jam, jump, and other words. She can print a *j* and you can finish the word that you or she thinks of.

Build her awareness of other sounds besides the *j* in these words.

All this is done without ever using the name "jay" for the letter. You can play with words in this manner for quite some time in the life of your child, not always with her name, but sometimes with words from a book such as *The Cat in the Hat*, or with any word that catches her fancy.

That is Step 2 in teaching reading: teach the forms and sounds of a few letters. Notice that you have bypassed learning the alphabet and learning the letter names. You have moved directly to the skill needed in sounding out words. It won't hurt Jenny if she learns the alphabet and letter names from watching television or from other children. She eventually will need to know them. But now in the beginning, you can strip reading down to its essentials. This makes it an exciting mental challenge—a matter of understanding and not just a matter of memorizing a lot of phonics facts that Jenny is not ready to use yet.

With one or two vowels and with a few consonants now in your pupil's head, she is ready for the next step, which is the most crucial point in her reading career. Be sure you understand the concept in Step 3 so you will recognize when your child has attained it.

Activities for Step 2

1. Ask the child to look around the room and see what else she can find that begins like *pan*. (Paper, pencil, popcorn, etc.) Look out the window and see what she can find that begins like s-s-sidewalk.

2. For an active child, let her jump up two stairsteps when she names a word in the game above. She jumps two more steps when she names another. How high can she get?

3. Print sounds onto cards. Place three or four cards in a row and say each sound, having your child say them after you. Then say, "Listen to me now and stop me when I make a mistake."

Reading

When the child "catches" you in a mistake, start at the beginning again and make a mistake in a different place. At first you may make absurd mistakes, such as a motorcycle sound or a dog's bark. Later, make the wrong letter sound. Mix the cards and repeat.

4. Hide a sound (letter) card behind a blank card. Slowly pull it upward and see how soon your child can tell which sound is coming up the elevator.

5. Place each sound you are teaching on a page of a scrapbook. Have the child look for pictures which begin with that sound.

6. Place a "sound for the day" or "sound for the week" on your child's bulletin board or on the refrigerator. During the day add words or pictures that match. Add fun by starting with a picture or real object such as a stuffed animal. Call it kangaroo day when you work on /k/ sound and panda day when you work on /p/ sound.

7. Have the child make place cards for the family dinner table. She may print only the first sound or, if she can, the full names.

STEP 3: Blending

During Step 2 you did not teach all the letters or all their sounds. That's the dull, memorizing, way of teaching. Your goal, instead, was to start your child toward the exciting discovery that the sounds blend together to make words. That discovery, itself, is Step 3.

When your child knows a few consonants and one or two vowels quite well, you can begin working on Step 3—blending. Let's say, for instance, that he has learned the short sound of *a*, which we will write here as /ă/. That is the sound of *a* as in dad.

Many people teach only the short sound of a vowel at first. And later when the child can blend well, they introduce additional sounds. This makes sense for two reasons. The first reason is that it minimizes the child's memory task. With only a few letters and sounds he can actually "read" by blending sounds together into words. And he is not confused with a lot of other sounds in his memory that he is not using yet. It's another shortcut; it gets you directly to the heart of the task.

A second reason for teaching the short sound first, is that it is used more often. For instance, when *a* is found in words, 70% of the time it sounds like /ă/, 25% of the time it sounds like /ay/, and about 5% of the time it sounds like /ah/. There are a few other sounds for *a*, but these three are the major ones, and all that a beginner needs to learn.

So now, let's suppose that your Johnny knows short *o* and short *a* sounds. And he knows a few consonant sounds: /n/ because it is in his name, and /p/ and /t/ because you made a point to teach them. To start this blending lesson, use only one vowel and print it on a chalkboard or paper above the consonants thus:

a

n p t

Point to the *a* and say /ă/ (the short sound as in dad). Teach Johnny to say /ă/ each time you point to it. Then slide your finger or pointer from *a* to *n*, and say the word *an*. Have Johnny say the word each time you point to those two sounds. Teach the word *at* in the same way. He may *say* the words, print them, and point them out for you to say. Practice in many ways. Point out *an* and *at* alternately and see if Johnny reads them correctly.

Try *ap*, too. No, that's not a word, you may tell Johnny. But it says *ap* anyway.

In this lesson or in future lessons, move on to three-letter words. Teach Johnny to blend sounds together to make words such as nap, pan, tan, Nat, Nan, tat. He should practice in these ways: read words when you point, point for you to read, write words, read words he writes, and read words you write.

One day add another letter. It can be a vowel or consonant. For instance, add *o* to make several new words: not, pot, top, tot, pop.

As your chart grows, keep vowels on top and consonants on the bottom. When you need other spellings of a sound, add them below the first spelling. For instance, if you need *ck* for the name Jack, add that below a *k*. After a few weeks your chart may look like this.

a o i

m n p t s j k

nn   ck

Blending skill is one of those things you cannot hurry in children. You can't sternly shake your finger at Johnny or promise him cake if he gets it right. All you can do is give him opportunities to learn it, and one day you will see he is beginning to catch on. That's a great day. The major hurdle to reading is about to be crossed. Nurture his beginning skill. Help it grow.

During this time, use other opportunities, also, to teach the blending skill. For instance, while reading stories to Johnny, find a word or two that he can sound out himself. Stories like *The Cat in the Hat* are gold mines for this stage of reading.

If the blending skill is slow in coming, your best approach is to spend more time on "real stuff" for a while and less time on reading instruction. Later, when your child seems ready, you can return to the blending lessons. Remember the "science" children in the research study? They turned out to be better readers in the end.

Activities for Step 3

1. Basic activities are for the child to: 1) say a word or syllable when you point it out on the chart, 2) say and write what you point out, 3) point out a word or syllable for you to read. (The chart is the row of vowels and the row of consonants which is described above.)

2. How many pronounceable ways can the child arrange a particular group of sounds you point out to her? For instance, *a*, *p*, and *t* can be arranged as *pat*, *tap*, and *apt*.

3. Point out words on the chart and have the child write each, in turn, on paper. Then copy each of her words neatly onto a card. Play one or more of these games with the cards. 1) As she reads each card to you she gets to jump one step up the stairs. As she reads through the pile a second time, she jumps back down. 2) Scramble the words on the floor or table. Read them one at a time and have the child find each word you read and hand it to you. 3) Spread out the cards, face up. Point out one of the words, sound by sound, on the chart. Have the child find and give you the word card which matches. Continue until you have all the

cards. 4) Switch places. Let the child be "teacher" and point out words for you to give her.

4. Print one vowel on each of five cards of one color. (Or fewer cards if your pupil does not know all the short sounds yet.) Use another color to make several consonant cards. Turn the cards face down, mix them up, and spread them out. Let the child draw three cards and see if she can make a word. She scores a point or wins an M&M or raisin if she does. Mix the cards again and take another turn. She should eventually learn to draw one vowel card and two consonant cards and try to make a word with the vowel in the middle. Some few words may take another pattern.

5. A more elaborate version of the above game is to cover dice or blocks with tape and print letters on the tape. Make one block for vowels, using *a* twice, and make two blocks for consonants. On each consonant block, print *p*, *t*, *m*, *n*, *b*, and *f*. Roll the dice and form a word before a timer runs out or before you count to twenty. After this game becomes easy for your child, change one of the consonant blocks to include other sounds, such as *r*, *d*, *j*, *h*, *w*, and *l*.

STEP 4: Decoding

If you have taught Johnny or Jenny how to blend sounds into words, give yourself a big reward. You earned it. And don't worry about the rest of the reading steps. It's all downhill from here.

Downhill but guidance is needed.

In Step 4, you at last do the things that many people think of as the beginning of reading. You teach all the letters and their sounds. You teach letter combinations such as *ck* and *th*. If Jenny hasn't already picked up the letter names and alphabetical order, you may teach those now, too.

Why were these matters delayed until Step 4? For two important reasons. First, it is mentally stimulating for Jenny. She has a place in her mind now to put this new information. Letters and sounds are not in a dull memorized list that she can't use. But she adds them to the growing reading plan, or scheme, in her head. Second, it is efficient. When she learns a new sound now, she puts it immediately to work and reinforces her new learning. Thus she learns more easily and quickly than she would have before.

The term "optimum learning time" applies to this procedure of teaching the letters and sounds after a child knows how to use them. When you wait for the optimum time, things go easier, faster, and better.

Now if your Jenny has caught on to the idea of blending sounds together, she is ready for Step 4. There is a lot to do in Step 4. But don't panic; it's easier than Step 3.

Before we describe the things to accomplish in this step, let's review some important teaching principles.

1. Teach each new item several times and in a variety of ways. Do not expect a child to learn something just because you told her once. She will occasionally, but don't depend on it for the long list of sounds you must now teach.

2. Proceed only as fast as the child can comfortably learn. Do not overload and discourage her.

3. Use both "look and say" and "write and say" methods with the phonics. Be sure your child writes every day. First, words; later, sentences.

4. Make sure your child experiences success in every lesson. If you've been working on something that's too hard, then turn to an easier task before stopping work for the day.

5. Review often.

Step 4 is phonics teaching, or decoding, as teachers often say nowadays. Many people are scared of phonics. So much has been written and spoken and researched by "experts," that parents have been intimidated.

Don't you be intimidated. Realize, first of all, that phonics is not "neat." The reason you feel you have never quite mastered phonics is that nobody's system completely wraps up the loose ends for you. Each system has a different way of weaving strands together, and each has different kinds of ends left loose. So it's only natural to feel that you can't answer all the questions that may come up while you're teaching.

But you read, don't you? Somehow, by yourself or with help, you picked up enough phonics knowledge to be able to read. Phonics is no mystery. You use it every day.

Adopt a commonsense attitude that you can teach phonics as well as the next person. It doesn't matter a great deal in what order you teach the items. Far more important is a warm relationship with your pupil and a happy atmosphere surrounding reading. If you want to buy flashcards and workbooks and charts,

VOWEL CHART

Vowels

a = cat, tame, want
e = pet, me (This vowel can change other vowel
      sounds: hat to hate, bit to bite.)
i = sit, hi
o = on, no, do
u = sun, cute, put
w = sometimes acts in a vowel pair: saw, few
y = funny, try

Vowels with r

er, ir, or, ur = /er/ as in her, sir, work, hurt
ar = car
or = for

Vowel pairs

ai, ay = rain, may (*y* at end of a word or syllable)
au, aw = fault, saw (*w* at end)
ea = eat, bread, break
ee = see
ei, ey = weigh, they; ceiling, key (*y* at end of
      words)
eu, ew = feud, few (*w* at end)
ie = piece, pie
oa, oe = boat, hoe (first vowel sounds, long)
oi, oy = boil, boy (slides from one sound to the
      next)
oo = too, took
ou, ow = loud, cow (slides)
ue, ui = blue, suit (after *g* the *i* is sounded: guitar,
      guide)

Reading

CONSONANT CHART

Consonants with one sound		Consonants with more than one sound	
b	= bat	c	= cat, cent
f	= fan	d	= dog, liked /t/, education /j/
h	= hat		
j	= jam	g	= get, gem /j/
k	= kit	s	= sat, has /z/, sure /sh/
l	= lad	x	= box /ks/, exact /gs/, anxiety /z/
m	= man		
n	= nap		
p	= pan	qu	= quack, plaque
r	= ran		
t	= tan		
v	= van		
w	= win		
y	= yes		
z	= zoo		

Consonant pairs (new sounds)		Consonant pairs (one letter silent)	
ch	= chip, chorus, chevron	ck	= back
gh	= enough (at end of words)	gh	= ghost (at beginning of words)
ng	= bang	gn	= gnaw
ph	= phone	kn	= know
sh	= ship	mb	= lamb
th	= this, thin	rh	= rhyme
wh	= why	wr	= write

(In other consonant pairs, such as *st*, *br*, and *ld*, both consonants have their regular sounds.)

fine. Anything on the market will help if you and your child enjoy working with the materials. Ignore the arguments about which system is best, because you're going to use an individualized system with your child. You're going to proceed at her pace. You're going to answer her questions, which may mean teaching some matters "out of order" according to a phonics system. So buy whatever you want or whatever is at hand. Or don't buy phonics materials at all. Use the money, instead, for good books.

The consonant and vowel charts will help you plan. Start with single-letter spellings. Add the others at whatever pace your child can learn them. You can teach a sound by simple homespun means. Use paper and crayon or pencil. Use a slate if you have one. Homemade flashcards work just as well as commercial ones. Show and say a sound, have Jenny say and write it. Read and write words which contain the sound. Review on the following days. That's all there is to it.

The two charts contain only seven lists, an entirely manageable number. If you wanted lists of every oddity of spelling you might encounter, the charts could be much longer, of course. But the great secret of phonics, which few dare to speak about, is that the child doesn't have to learn it all. That's right, and it's not heresy; it's only common sense. The time comes when it is more convenient for the child simply to learn the words than to learn obscure phonics rules.

For instance, you could teach the six sounds of *ough*, and when your pupil comes to the word *thought* she can try to decide which of the six sounds to say. But how cumbersome! It is much simpler just to learn the word *thought*, and to learn other "rough and tough" words: *though, through, cough, bough,* and *enough*. This is the same as learning phonics, because from each word the child can figure out others. For instance, from the word *thought* she can figure out *bought, brought,* and *fought*. In fact, in this case it works better than starting with *ough*. She is, in effect, starting with *ought*, and that has only one pronunciation and not six.

As you teach, you will bump into the messiness of phonics many times over. Say that Jenny needs help with the word *might*. Do you tell her that it's the second sound of *i*, /eye/, and a silent *gh*? Or do you tell her that *igh* says /eye/? Well, it doesn't matter which you tell her, because if she can read *might* she can figure out *fight*, *sight*, *bright*, *sigh*, and so forth.

Here is another messiness. What do you do with words like *motion, gracious,* and *passion*? You could teach a rule that *t, c,* and *s*, when followed by *i*, have a /sh/ sound. That's partly true. Sometimes *si* has a /zh/ sound, as in *vision*. On the other hand, you could just let Jenny learn the whole second syllable in the words mentioned. That will help her figure out numerous words that end similarly.

As a general principle, then, when you bump into a messy phonics problem, you can just teach the syllable or word at hand. That will be useful for your child, in many cases more useful than if you teach some obscure phonics rule that covers the situation.

This in essence is the great unadvertised secret of phonics. You don't have to continue until every last phonics rule and obscure sound is mastered. You can start off systematically teaching a list of sounds. But at some point your child will take off and fly with her reading skills. She forms her own rules and doesn't need the rest that you planned to teach. Let her fly.

Sight Words

Some words of high use are not phonetically regular. It saves time to let the child simply learn these as sight words instead of trying to learn all the phonics they require. These words, in alphabetical order, are:

any	one	some
come	other	the
could	people	there
from	said	two
many	says	was
of	should	would

By grouping the sight words, you can simplify the learning. task for your child. One group is:

could	should	would

In another group, *o* has the sound of /uh/. If you wish, you can teach that as a fourth sound of *o*. *One* (and *once*) could be added to the group. In these two words *o* has the sound of /wuh/. This group is:

come	of	other
from	one	some

In a third group *a*, as well as *ai* and *ay*, has the sound /eh/. This group is:

any	said	says
many		

This leaves only five words to learn separately. They are:

people	there	was
the	two	

Early in Step 4, you can test your child on the above words by having her read from the list any that she knows. Make flashcards for the rest of the words—those she doesn't know—and practice them daily. Have her practice writing the words, also. If writing is a struggle for her, use short phrases such as "one ball," "two balls;" "the cat," "any cat." Later, when writing becomes easier, she should write full sentences and even paragraphs.

Reading

Writing

Writing skill and reading skill grow together. Writing, in fact, is a powerful method to use in your teaching. To write, Jenny must totally concentrate. Eye, hand, and brain are used. Mental hearing and speech are involved. And if you dictate or she reads what is to be written, then actual hearing and speech are involved. Even a few minutes of writing each day will greatly enhance the learning of reading.

How do you teach writing? At earlier steps you probably wrote (printed) Jenny's name and let her trace it. This is a good way to start. Next, instead of tracing, she can copy. Later, when an image is formed in her head, she can copy from this mental image. That is, she will be able to write some words without looking at a model.

Now in Step 4, use all these teaching methods: 1) write models for the child to copy, 2) dictate models for the child to write, and 3) let the child make up her own writings. Each method is explained more fully in the following sections.

1) Copying. Print one or more full sentences for the child to copy. Be careful to use capital and small letters accurately. Teach about capitals at the beginning of sentences and periods or other marks at the end. Sources for sentences are many. You or the child can make them up or you can find them in books, poems, or songs. Try "I'll huff and I'll puff and I'll blow your house in," or "You can't catch me. I'm the gingerbread man." Use the copying method daily at first. When your child becomes proficient at copying, use the method of dictating more and more often.

2) Dictating. Dictate sentences for the child to write. From your voice inflections she must decide how to punctuate. Also she must decide about capitalizations and spellings. After she writes, give her immediate feedback by letting her see the original that you dictated from. Learn from each error. Fold back her first try and let her try again if she thinks she can do better. After she becomes proficient at writing sentences from dictation, move on to paragraphs and longer selections. Dictating from good books definitely does NOT stifle creativity. It gives your child more tools and more skill with which to be creative. Use this method regularly—at least twice a week.

3) Writing. Some children need no urging to write a story of their own, and others need much help and encouragement. So you can use more of method 3 (writing) or more of method 2 (dictating) according to the preferences of your particular pupil. Most teachers are agreed that learning proceeds better if you are not overly critical of the child's efforts at this early time in her writing career. The problems of sentence construction, spelling, punctuation, and so forth are too much to master all at once. Let the child write freely. Tell her how to spell any word she asks for. Let her spell others phonetically, even though wrong. Afterward, enjoy her story. Commend her. And make your private notes about what to teach in a future phonics or spelling lesson or other lesson.

Spelling

To teach writing you naturally need to include spelling. For the most efficient home teaching, spelling should be integrated with reading, phonics, and writing lessons. Studying lists from a spelling book is less efficient.

There are two approaches you can take to spelling. One is the phonics approach. As you teach a new sound, write, read, and spell some words which use that sound. For instance, when you are teaching the first sound of *x*, list some words that end with that sound: *fox, box, fix, mix, ax,* and so forth. If your pupil can handle harder words, try ones like *axle, extra,* and *excuse.* Spelling tests on "families" like this are fun and not too difficult. After a few families have been studied, have a test on words

Reading

from several families. This shows if one of them might need some reviewing.

Here are some additional spelling helps which do not appear in the phonics charts. You may use these, also, for teaching spelling by the phonics approach.

1. In a syllable or word with consonant-vowel-consonant pattern, the vowel is usually short. Examples: cat, win.

2. When a single vowel ends a syllable or word, it is usually long. Examples: go, he.

NOTE: Both 1 and 2 often help you decide whether a consonant is double or not. For example: lit-tle, bri-dle. In the word *little,* the short vowel sound indicates that two *t*'s are needed, one to enclose the vowel in the first syllable and one to start the next syllable. The long vowel sound in *bridle* tells you that it should not be enclosed with an extra *d.*

3. *I* before *e* except after *c* or when sounded like /ay/ as in *neighbor* or *weigh.*

4. Change *y* to *i* before adding an ending (when the *y* is preceded by a consonant). Examples: babies, funniest, but monkeying.

5. Drop silent *e* and add *ing* or other endings which begin with a vowel.

6. When a final consonant is preceded by one vowel, double the consonant before adding *ing* or other endings which begin with a vowel. This works with one-syllable words and with words accented on the last syllable. Examples: running, runner; beginning, but deepening.

7. On longer words, spell one syllable at a time, using whatever phonics guidelines help in each syllable.

A powerful method for teaching is to help the child figure out rules by herself. For instance, to help Jenny learn the silent *e* rule which is on the vowel chart, begin with a list of words with short vowel sounds, as in the first column below.

hat	hate
can	cane
hop	hope
bit	bite
cut	cute

Lead her to see that each word has a short vowel sound, as she probably learned previously. Then tell her to copy one of the words, add a silent *e* to it, and read her new word. Continue with more of the words, as in the second column above. Then see if she can make up a rule to explain what silent *e* does to words.

Practically everything you teach in phonics or spelling can be approached in this way, with the child figuring out things for herself. Advantages of this method are: 1) you can see whether the child understands and is not just repeating by rote, 2) the child learns thinking skills that help with future problems as well as the one at hand, 3) it results in faster learning for the child and less reteaching for you.

A second approach to spelling is called the "common word" approach. Spelling texts using this system have weekly lists of words selected from larger lists, such as "The 1000 Most Commonly Used Words." This is a convenient way to teach a classroom full of children. But there's a more efficient way to do it at home. You and your child can collect weekly lists of words from your child's own daily writing. This individualized system saves her the time of studying and being tested on words someone else in a class needs but she already knows. And it will naturally include any words in "The 1000 Most Commonly Used Words" that she can't spell yet. If a word is common, she will be using it. If she doesn't use it, it's not very common.

For a strong spelling program, use both the phonics approach and the common word approach. Mix them in any arrangement. This week have a list of words in a phonics "family." Next week use a list collected from your child's writings. Or after you collect a number of words, arrange some of them into phonics families for easier learning.

Teach handwriting along with spelling. After your child has good control of a pencil, use lined paper and insist upon correct forms for all letters. Let her continue manuscript writing (printing) for a couple of years, or until she writes quite easily and rapidly. Then you may let her switch to cursive writing. Only a few weeks are needed for the change if you wait for the optimum time.

Step 4 may last for many months or even two or three years. For some few children, most decoding skills can be mastered in a few weeks. Step 4 involves more work on your part than the next step. You must teach phonics more or less systematically. You must see that the child reads and writes every school day. It is important, also, to enjoy books with your child. Continue reading to her. Laugh together over funny books. Wonder together at the marvelous things you find in books. Gradually your child will arrive at Step 5.

Activities for Step 4

1. Activities 1, 2, and 3 given for Step 3 may each be extended now to include more sounds.

2. Start a notebook. Add pages gradually, as new sounds and phonics rules are studied. Either make one page for each consonant and vowel, and later for the pairs, or make pages with clusters of sounds, and rules governing them. For instance, a page could list the consonants that have only one sound and another page list the consonants with more than one sound. A later page could have all the vowel pairs that begin with *a*. Refer to the pages for review. Add examples and rules whenever new information is learned.

3. When the child is learning a new sound-spelling, such as *ar*, you and she can collect a list of spelling words using the sound. (Car, start, mark, dart, alarm, farm, march.) Test her on the list. After several such lists are collected, give a test using selected words from all the lists. Review as needed.

4. Develop a dictionary or a file of spelling bears—words which are difficult to remember because they are not phonetically regular. Add to the dictionary whenever you stumble across such a word in the day's reading or writing lesson. Periodically study a group of these and take a test on them. Don't let the list become unmanageably long. If it threatens to, weed out words that seem less useful than others.

5. Print a phonics family of words in a row or other formation and let the child read them to "swim across the river," "walk the tightrope," "go up the elevator," or "ride the roller coaster." Example, the *ng* family: *sing, bang, hang, ring, hung, ping, pong, lung, rang, sang*. For a more active version of this activity, print the words on cards and let the child jump up the stairsteps or walk along a balance beam as he reads each word.

6. Play a more difficult version of game 4 in the Step 3 section. Draw three consonant cards and one vowel card. If the child can make a word with all four cards she wins four M&M's. If she uses only two or three cards she wins 2 or 3 M&M's. Four-letter words will usually be in the pattern of *fast* or of *stop*. That is, the vowel appears in second or third position and two consonants blend together either before or after the vowel.

STEP 5: Fluency

Let this step overlap the previous one, as all the steps do. When your child knows the consonant sounds and the common vowel sounds and is beginning to learn about the pairs, start providing him with as much easy reading material as you can find. Let him read, read, read.

Don't be a pushy parent who forces a child into harder books than he wants. Easy books give Johnny opportunity to consolidate his knowledge and skill in the decoding matters. Easy books also help him learn and overlearn the common words in our language that are used repeatedly. These common words make up a large percentage of the vocabulary even in difficult books. But let Johnny practice them in easy books. Easy books help him gain skills in smooth and rapid reading. They stimulate his thinking and his imagination. He also learns that books are fun. When he is not struggling with difficult vocabulary, he can occupy his mind with the content of stories and books. And even at this easy level, wide vistas of information, ideas, and attitudes begin to open up for him.

But remember, gaining information from books is not the main purpose during this step. That comes later. The main purpose now is to read, read, read, so that decoding skills become overlearned and automatic.

What about comprehension? If you have followed any debates on reading instruction, you probably have heard that you should be teaching something called "comprehension." Some people even say that you shouldn't teach so much phonics; you should be teaching comprehension, instead. But don't worry about that. If your child laughs at something in a book, he is comprehending it. If he asks a question, he is thinking and comprehending. If he sometimes chooses his own books, on dinosaurs or whatever, he is comprehending. The point the "comprehension" people miss is that the child uses easy books during his early steps in reading. Of course he comprehends them.

The truth in this debate, as you have no doubt seen, is that phonics has its place in the early stages of reading, and comprehension can be emphasized later. Just now, in Step 5, your child should gain fluency. This is a step that many people try to skip. They keep pushing on to the hard stuff.

As was mentioned earlier, you may let this step overlap with Step 4. So that means you are still carrying on systematic phonics lessons. Teach the consonant and vowel pairs one at a time. Also teach any other phonics that your child bumps into in his reading. This individualized teaching may not seem very systematic, but it is highly efficient. When Johnny meets a problem and you help him solve it, that is a strong learning episode. The item will require less reteaching and less review. So that is a "system" of teaching phonics. It is a powerful method, individualized, and especially suited for home teaching.

Here is a list of basic activities your child can do during this step. Using all of them from time to time will give variety to your lessons.

Spell words from dictation.
Copy sentences from your model.
Write sentences from dictation.
Find a particular word or sentence that you read from a page.
From a page, find the answer to a question that you ask.
Read aloud with good expression.
Read silently, tell about the story, then read aloud.
Write an original story.
Draw a picture to illustrate the original story.

Learn a new phonics rule when an unusual word is encountered.

Listen to you read stories.

Also, for variety from time to time, you can use game and activity ideas in Step 4, as well as the new activities given at the end of this Step 5 section.

Evaluating Your Child's Reading

When you work with your child daily, you should feel little need to test him. You know how well he reads orally. You know what decoding skills you have tried to teach but he still forgets. You know if he is plunging on ahead, not seeming to need any more phonics. The truth is, you know more about his reading than most tests will tell you.

But one question still lurks in the back of many parents' minds. They want to know how Johnny compares with other children his age. Comparisons are a bit tricky, because there is wide variation in the abilities of children of any particular age or grade. And they are really not as helpful as other concepts about reading levels. But this evaluation section will suggest some simple, informal ways to compare your child's reading with average grade levels. It also will suggest a second concept of reading levels which you will use practically every teaching day.

The second concept is to understand that your child has three reading levels at all times. These have been called his 1) independent level, 2) instructional level, and 3) frustration level. This is more a way to rate books than to rate Johnny. The books Johnny can read by himself are on his independent level. The books you might use to teach him new skills are on his instructional level. And the books too hard even for that are at his frustration level.

Like Goldilocks, you might say, "This book is to-o-o hard.

This book is to-o-o easy. But this book is ju-u-st right." You can teach Johnny to identify books too hard for him. But the other levels are only for your planning, not for his. No child ever says, "This book is to-o-o easy," all on his own. If spoken at all, it is from a child of pushy parents, a child who has heard remarks about him reading baby books. This is not a natural reaction to books. We adults don't pick up a "Reader's Digest" and say, "This is to-o-o easy." The fact is, we probably pick it up at the end of a busy day because we want some easy, relaxing reading. Let Johnny have that same privilege of reading for enjoyment. In this fluency step of reading, you want him to read lots of easy books.

To determine whether a book is too hard, count off a section of 100 words and ask the child to read it to you. If he is unable to read more than five of the words, the book is on his frustration level. He can be taught a form of this test, himself, as a useful means of selecting library books. He simply reads a page and counts on his fingers the words he does not know. If he runs out of fingers on one hand, including his thumb, the book is likely to be harder than he wants. This system assumes that the page will have from 100 to 200 words on it.

If the child misses from three to five words on your 100 word sample, you may consider the book to be on his instructional level. It is just right. Never assume that the harder a book is, the more a child can learn from it. A book that stretches and challenges, but does not frustrate, is the best choice for teaching.

You can test further, by asking questions about the sample selection. Keeping score on questions is more complicated, but you can learn to estimate. If the word count indicates you have a book on the instructional level, try asking a few questions. If the child answers about three out of four, this confirms the diagnosis. It shows he understands a lot of what he reads, but there is still room for you to teach something.

Reading

For your quick reference, a chart of this testing procedure follows.

	Words Missed	Questions Missed
Independent reading level:	0 to 2%	up to 10%
Instructional reading level:	3 to 5%	up to 25%
Frustration reading level:	over 5%	over 25%

It may take a little time to clearly understand what those levels are all about. But try scoring some library books or even some of your child's textbooks and see what the scores tell you. If textbooks are at his frustration level, this will explain the trouble he's been having.

After you have in your head a good picture of the above levels, move on to this next concept, called the "expectancy level." This is a highly significant concept understood by relatively few people. It tells whether your child is doing as well as you should expect him to.

Wouldn't you give a lot for that information? If you knew your child should be doing better, you would start looking for the problem. Does he need more phonics? Does he need a better attitude and more time spent on reading? Does he need the help of a skilled opthamologist or other professional? You would find the trouble, remedy it, and bring the child up to his expectancy level. On the other hand, if you find he is reading up to expectancy level already, you can relax. If you've been pushing, you can slow down and allow him more time to grow into advanced reading levels.

To find the expectancy level, you can use the same 100 word samples you counted off for the child to read. Or similar samples will do. But this time you read aloud to the child. Then ask him about the meaning of words in the selection. Also ask other questions. And score exactly as in the chart above. You now know whether the child has vocabulary enough and understanding enough to read a particular book. If the score shows that you should "expect" him to read the book, but he can't, then you have a teaching problem to solve. If the score shows that he doesn't understand the book even when you read it to him, then don't expect him to read it . . . yet.

With the concept of expectancy, you sometimes can get useful information from an achievement test the child takes at school. Some of these tests, in the subheadings under "reading," have a score for a test in which the teacher read the words. Ask about each subhead, and if you find one like this, treat it as an expectancy score. For example, if your child scored fourth grade level in that subtest but only third grade level in reading overall, you may suspect that he needs more phonics or something to bring his reading up to the expectancy level.

Now we turn to the tricky concept of comparing your child's reading with grade levels. One simple way to do this is to use the same procedure as above, but do the testing from a series of graded reading textbooks. Borrow the books from your local school or from the public library. If your child is third grade age, for instance, you should get readers from first grade, second grade, and so on up for as high as you think he may be able to read. Use 100 word samples from the middle of each book and test as described above to find which book meets his instructional level.

This gives you a rough idea of how far the child has progressed. But the tricky part is that it doesn't tell you what grade he should be in. That's because in any fourth grade, for instance, some children will read at first or second grade level and others may read at eighth grade level or even higher. What is called "fourth grade level" really is just a point at the middle of the class. So if your child is fourth grade age but scores about third

Reading

grade on reading tests, that doesn't mean he flunked fourth grade. It just means he is below the middle. Everybody can't be above the middle. Only half the class can be there.

If your fourth grader scores sixth grade level, it doesn't mean he should be promoted to sixth grade where he would be at the middle. Let him stay in fourth and be above the middle. If you are teaching him at home, you should get more challenging books, though, in subjects requiring reading. That, of course, is an advantage of tutoring individually at home. You can more easily adapt the teaching to fit the child.

It is best not to concern yourself much with testing until at least third grade. In the first two grades children can score quite differently on tests depending on whether they are learning by a phonics method or by a sight word method. Also, in the first two grades children often need pauses for consolidation of their learning. They may pause and spurt at different times. During summer vacation after first grade, children forget a lot that must be reviewed and relearned the next year. And children are not all ready to begin reading at the same age. All these variables make it unwise to test young children and compare them with other children or with a grade level. When states or local school districts require testing of homeschooled children, they often are flexible with young children and will postpone testing if you request it.

If you have gone through the five steps in this guide, if your child can blend sounds together, has learned quite a lot of phonics, and has spent time gaining fluency, then you might wish to test or have some professional testing done. If you do, use the test results wisely. They are not a club to beat your child with. They are not to brag to friends about. The only sensible use is to gain information that might be helpful in planning future lessons for the child.

Activities for Step 5

1. Plan regular trips to the library with your child and treat these occasions as high-level family outings. You can go off to choose books for yourself while the child attends a story hour or plays with puppets or chooses his books. Take home some easy books he will read himself, one or two harder ones you will read to him, and perhaps a science book which he cannot read but which has beautiful pictures to learn from. On the way home stop for ice cream or pizza or whatever rates high in your family. Back home again, the next reading lesson is "free reading," in which the child is allowed time to simply read for fun from his new library selections. It's all right if he rejects a book once he starts reading it. We adults do that all the time.

2. Now and then, when your budget can stand it, take a family excursion to a bookstore. Let your child grow up learning that families buy books as well as records and sports equipment and other recreational items.

3. Prepare your child to get the most out of a book. This means, whenever possible, you will read it first. (You can learn to skin rapidly through most children's books, so this is not an impossible addition to your schedule.) If the book is set in another country or in the long ago or is about an unfamiliar subject, tell him a little about these matters. Introduce him to new words and ideas he will encounter in the book, not so much preteaching that you spoil the book for him, but just enough to strengthen and direct his interest.

4. While you are reading a book to the child, occasionally ask what he thinks will happen next. Why? Discuss the characters. Does the child like each person? Why or why not? Does he like the way the story ends? When you read the same stories your child does, you will find opportunities to talk about values that are important in the life of your family. This, perhaps, is the main reason you are teaching the child at home. Be careful, though, not

Reading

to belabor these matters. Use a light touch, and only some of the books.

5. On family trips, arrange time to stop at factories, mines, or other businesses and ask about tours. Even those which don't have regular tours are often happy to show off for interested people. Museums, botanical gardens, and other public places are also good for extending your child's learning, especially when taken in small bites. All new experiences extend your child's vocabulary and knowledge and make him a better reader. On trips, also, don't pass up the many opportunities to learn map reading.

6. Don't wait for vacations, but plan mini-trips close to home. Will a friend in the bank take your child to see a vault? Is there a slough nearby where water backs up from a river? And for extending vocabulary, what about the baking powder, garlic buds, furnace filters, or carburetor around your house and garage? Have you dried dandelion roots and crushed them for tea? Opportunity for learning new words is endless. In fact, you can hardly stop your child from learning them. Just don't keep him bent over spelling papers, vocabulary workbooks, and difficult books. Let him freely learn from real life.

7. The child may read aloud to a younger sibling or friend. If you can pull this off, he will be reviewing the fun and phonics of nursery rhymes and other "babyish" literature that he might not read otherwise.

8. Sometimes when your child makes up stories of his own, especially when he has a long story, write it for him. Let him dictate while you get it down. Use a typewriter or word processor if you have one. Later, share the stories with someone. Have them read at the family dinner table; mail some to Grandma or a friend. Authors need an audience.

9. Make occasions for letter writing. Have the child write to a relative, send for free samples or for mail order items, write

to a newspaper or the mayor about a current controversy, write to a TV station to give opinions about their programing.

10. Help the child make a book about one of his hobbies. Each page, for instance, might describe one of the rocks in his collection and remind him about where and how he found it.

A Final Word

Finally, congratulations are due to you for taking your child up the steps from prereading through decoding and fluency. Your greater reward is that your child has as fine a start in reading as he could get anywhere. He now has learned to read. From this point on, he can read to learn. A path toward a richer, more meaningful life for him now leads into the years ahead.

A Strong Start in LANGUAGE

Contents

Writing

The Powerful
Natural Method

Parent, you may not realize it, but you are an excellent language teacher. You can prove that by the speech of your child. Think of how much language he learned by age five or so. Don't you wish you spoke a new foreign language as well? If you did, you could go to that country and ask directions, make purchases, or get acquainted with people. In short, you would feel fairly competent in the language.

That's the amazing accomplishment of your young child. How did you teach him? By using the powerful natural method. This manual will show you how to extend the natural method from spoken language to written language. With this method your child's writing ability will grow in great leaps, just as his speaking ability grew in the preschool years.

The method is not new or experimental. It is an old and proven method, probably as old as writing itself. Great writers have used it, and you have already used it with your child. But once children reach school age, we tend to shed the natural method for a slower, artificial method. Our society thinks grammar books or language books somehow carry the secret of good writing, but few of them do.

What is the natural method of learning to write? Before defining it, let's think back to the child's learning of speech. How did he learn to speak? By listening and speaking. The baby at first listened to you, he imitated sounds and words, and from there he rapidly grew into a competent speaker. This is no secret known only in the ivy halls of teacher colleges. It is known in every house on the block. And if that sounds like a miracle, attribute it to the innate abilities God planted in the child. Speech is learned by listening and speaking.

Now, what is the parallel for written language? It is reading and writing. We might state the analogy this way: Listening and speaking are to spoken language what reading and writing are to written language. If people ask you how children learn to write, here is the short, short definition to give them: Children learn to write by writing.

But you need a longer definition than that in order to make practical use of this powerful natural method in your teaching. For that, we must examine some features of this system.

What You Do in a Lesson

Probably your child's first writing lesson was when you printed his name and he traced it or copied it. Or maybe you started even earlier with one letter instead of a word. This kind of copying is what happens in many lessons for a young child. Later, the copying gives way to writing from dictation. Copying and dictating are the two basic lesson activities in the natural method. Just as the child learned to speak by copying your correct speech, so he learns to write by copying fine writing.

Jack London tells how he taught himself to write his famous adventure stories. Even if they had summer writing conferences in his day, he could not have afforded to go to one. But he stumbled onto the natural method, which obviously helped his career more than a conference would have anyway. London spent days upon days in the San Francisco Public Library hand copying good literature that the librarian recommended to him.

Benjamin Franklin tells in his autobiography how he taught himself to write. It began when he admired some writing in a British periodical, *The Spectator.* The essays with their closely reasoned arguments caught his fancy, and he wanted to write like that. So he outlined essays, put his outlines aside for a few days, and later tried to rewrite an original article by following his outline. He compared his writing with the model to see where he fell short. Then he repeated with the same essay again or tried another essay, improving his writing all the while. Later, he had the pleasure of thinking he sometimes did a portion better than the writer he was modeling.

These three examples indicate the broad range of levels you can use with your child when you plan writing lessons—all the way from carefully forming letters of a child's name to reconstructing an essay from an outline. Copy, dictate, compare, repeat. These and similar activities can be used in any combination in your daily writing lessons.

A caution is in order here: The natural method sounds simple in theory and your lessons may seem easy to plan, but do not be deceived. Writing is hard work. Some days your child will complain, "Do I have to write today?" "Yes," you should answer, "you have to write every day." That means every school day, except for field trip days or other occasions when writing gets squeezed out by something better.

The following list gives in brief the levels of difficulty from easy to hard that you can use in your lesson plans.

1. Trace a model letter or word.

2. Copy a model word or sentence.

3. Write a sentence from slow dictation, getting all the help necessary to make it correct.

4. Write a familiar sentence from dictation given at normal speed and expression. Compare. Write again.

5. Write an unfamiliar sentence from dictation. Compare. Write again.

6. Study a paragraph. Write as it is dictated sentence by sentence in normal expression. Compare and correct errors.

7. Write an unfamiliar paragraph from dictation, deciding

from the expression how it should be punctuated. Compare. Talk about any differences between your writing and the model. Learn from these differences.

8. Write from dictation a variety of passages which are longer than a paragraph—dialogues, descriptions, news stories, and others. Compare. Learn.

9. Review by repeating two or three times any lesson in which you made too many errors. (If you keep on making many errors, find easier sentences or paragraphs.)

10. Make notes on a passage of writing that you like, and put the notes away for a few days. Then try to rewrite the passage from your notes. Compare with the model. What did you do well? Where will you do better next time? Repeat, using the same model or a new one.

11. Find a description, or poem, or any short piece of writing that you like. Use it as a pattern to write something of your own.

12. Find a letter to the editor or other piece of writing that you disagree with. Write your answer.

13. When you have something to say, decide what form you will use—essay, poem, letter, or other—and write your thoughts for someone else to read.

You can see from this list that the range of difficulty can take you from kindergarten or first grade through the Benjamin Franklin level. Another way to vary the difficulty is through the choice of content for writing. For instance, number 11, which is high on the difficulty list, could be adapted to primary children by selecting a nursery rhyme or other model the child likes and letting him imitate it and try to make his own. Or for older writers, an existing set of by-laws could provide a model for writing by-laws for a new organization. Number 13, also, can be used by primary children or by their parents.

Thus, the levels should not be used too rigidly in your teaching. But they can give you general guidelines for helping your child progress in his writing.

Proven Track Record

Another feature of the powerful natural method of teaching writing is that it has a long proven track record. Not only did Jack London and Benjamin Franklin use it, but so also did countless other famous and ordinary writers of past generations.

Past generations of American students were raised on it. They wrote in more complex sentences and often with more organized thoughts because they studied from those kinds of models. In some places or eras of our past, children were tutored, and the natural method could easily be used. After schools grew large and graded, workbooks came into use as a way for teachers to manage large groups of children. And workbooks diluted the task of writing. Though the natural method could work well in classrooms, and does in some schools, filling in blanks too often substituted for real writing.

Now with a revival of home tutoring there is opportunity to discard workbooks and do real writing again. Mothers across the country are rediscovering the natural method. One mother read in a McGuffey reader that copying and dictating methods were good to use. She tried it and was amazed at the results. Her child, she said, could write anything he wanted to. Other mothers discover the method simply because it is the natural one. They start by showing a child to write his name, and go on from there.

So throughout American history, right up to the present day, many people have used and are using the natural method with excellent results. Those who are just hearing about it say, "It must be good because it sounds so sensible."

Writing

From Whole to Part

An old debate among curriculum makers involves the whole-versus-part question. Should you teach something piece by piece by piece until the pieces add up to a whole? Or should you start with some kind of understandable whole and teach the pieces through it? The reason the debate goes on so long is that neither method is right for every topic and for every time. The wholes and the parts do not separate as neatly as curriculum planners would like.

In language teaching, what is a whole? As the method is described in this manual, a whole is any meaningful piece of language—from a word or sentence up to an essay or even longer passage of writing. This is written language in its natural setting.

What are the parts of language? They are innumerable and include all kinds of grammar matters; punctuation, capitalization and other mechanics; usage; vocabulary; spelling; meaning; forms; and on and on.

Now, the big question is: Is it better to move from whole to parts or from parts to whole? The natural method, the method of learning to write by studying and doing writing, is basically a whole-to-part method.

Teaching of the grammar parts has been researched extensively. If you tested any group of children to find who knows a lot of grammar and who knows only a little grammar, you would find that the grammar scores do not correlate with quality of writing. Children who know the most grammar are not necessarily better writers. The parts do not add up to the desired whole.

But moving in the opposite direction does work. That is, students who are good writers can learn grammar better than students who are poor writers. Grammar is not a way to good writing; it is a tool that good writers use to analyze writing, to justify doing something this way instead of that way, and so forth.

When your child learned to speak, he learned more grammar

than you ever thought of teaching him. Even a five-year-old uses statements, questions, commands and exclamations. In other words, he knows the major types of sentences. He forms most sentences with subjects and predicates. He uses verbs in both present and past tense forms. Many other details of grammar could be added to the list. All this without a formal grammar lesson!

Children's mistakes can make us aware of how much grammar they have absorbed. "I knowed the cake was in there," shows that the child can form past tense by adding *ed* to a verb. The problem in the cake sentence is that the child hasn't learned yet about irregular verbs—at least the verb *know.*

One young preschooler said, "It isn't any more rain." If we were to correct him we might say, *"There* isn't any more rain." The words it and *there* are sometimes used in this manner as anticipatory subjects, in this case to anticipate the real subject, rain. *It* is also used as an impersonal pronoun, as in "It isn't raining any more." What sophisticated grammar this child almost had in his grasp!

The learning method which children use for spoken language works as well for written language. You can teach the parts of capitalization, punctuation, spelling, sometimes grammar, and numerous other matters day by day in the dictation and copying lessons. Some of them you will consciously teach. Many others the child will learn without your conscious effort. He will learn from the good language models he studies, in the same natural way he learned to speak.

Efficiency is a correlate of learning from wholes. When your child studies from a workbook or textbook in which parts chosen by a curriculum planner are laid out in some kind of order, it is inevitable that the child will meet parts he already knows or parts he cannot yet understand. It also is inevitable that he will learn some matters that he does not yet need in his writing, so he will forget them. When your child learns any part because he needs it to get his dictation correct, the learning is stronger.

A part-to-whole lesson on nouns, for instance, may teach a definition of nouns, list some nouns, and then give sentences for underlining the nouns. In this, the noun lesson is predominant and whatever meaning or significance the sentences may have is only incidental. But a whole-to-part lesson could begin with a paragraph from a history book which you chose because of its meaning and significance. Say that the child writes it from dictation and does well, so you decide to add on an incidental lesson about nouns. Discussing nouns in the passage gives an extra boost to vocabulary learning. You could notice proper nouns and titles, such as General Washington. In such a lesson, meaning is uppermost, and the noun learning incidental. But even in its incidental position it is stronger learning about nouns than in the other lesson.

In summary, a feature of the natural method is that it moves from whole to part. This kind of learning is stronger and more efficient. It is proven. It works.

Leads to Creativity

If you teach language by the natural method, sooner or later some friend is sure to say, "It stifles creativity to have the child write from models instead of using his own creative ideas." Our society is so obsessed with creativity that people want children to be creative before they have any knowledge or skill to be creative with. In using this natural method you will be providing your child with knowledge and skill. Whenever he has an idea for a story, poem, letter, or anything of his own, let him write it. Encourage such creative urges when they poke up their heads. But in between times, get back to the daily dictation lessons. There is no better way to give your child a strong foundation for his own creative writing.

Listen to a musician advising young composers how to learn from the great masters: "As a technical exercise he may copy down the soprano line . . . and attempt to supply the accompanying parts, comparing his result with that of the master. He will find that with practice he is able to duplicate the original accompaniments or supply alternatives which are equally proficient technically" (Harold Shapero in *The Creative Process* edited by Brewster Ghiselin). Does that sound like the Benjamin Franklin method of writing?

Every master painter had followers who painted imitations of his works as a way to become painters in their own right. That is why art lovers today sometimes have difficulty figuring out whether a particular painting is an original or a copy.

Your child should not be required to reinvent the wheel, so to speak, in learning to write. Let him learn from fine writing models; then his creativity can begin at higher levels. An occasional fifth grader has a novel in her head and at every opportunity sneaks out her manuscript to write a few more paragraphs. An occasional third or fourth grader keeps diaries without anyone assigning such a project. Many first graders, excited that they can now write and spell a few words, want to make up their own stories.

It works well to let children write their own material when they have something in their heads to write. But it does not work well to regularly require original writing. Too many school children have written "What I Did on My Summer Vacation" and "What I Would Do if I Had a Million Dollars."

The natural method frees you from having to find or think up writing topics to try to motivate your child to do original writing. It is relatively easy to find passages for copying and dictation. They can come from any reading lesson or from science, history, poetry—in fact, from anything meaningful to the child that you think is worth his time.

Writing

So you have an answer for friends who worry about creativity: "The natural method leads to higher levels of creativity than other methods."

Grade-Level Guidelines

The grade-level lists that follow are distilled from major language textbooks so you can see what the majority of schools purport to teach. I think they are good lists for homeschool guidance except for the grammar sections in second and third grades. It is better to wait until about seventh grade when children are fairly good writers, and then have some units on grammar.

In this advice, I am separating grammar from usage and from writing mechanics. Strictly speaking, grammar is the study of the parts of speech and the parts of sentences. As mentioned earlier, much research has shown that knowledge of grammar does not correlate at all with good writing. So reverse the order in your teaching. Teach your children first to write well and then teach them some grammar. They will understand it at that time, and may even enjoy it, not having been burned out previously with years of useless grammar study.

Young children should learn the mechanics. The mechanics are punctuation, capitalization and other details needed for writing but not needed for speaking.

If you delay grammar, don't worry about "gaps" or achievement tests, or keeping up with the schools. If your children are immersed in language—hearing and reading good books, conversing, and writing—they will do fine in the tests. No test asks them to underline a verb or to find a preposition. Any student with a good ear for language can answer the kinds of questions they will meet on the tests. And don't worry that your child is missing something he might have gotten in school. If you look in a textbook for some of the grammar items listed, you will find only one or two lessons on them. Or sometimes an item has no lesson, but is included briefly on a page that teaches another topic.

In other words, those scope and sequence charts seem primarily for impressing textbook selection committees, or maybe parents, and the curriculum writers know better than to teach a lot of grammar to primary children.

With the natural method, you will have no problem teaching the non-grammar items on these lists.

First Grade

Oral Language. Speak clearly. Show courtesy. Tell about something, keeping to the subject.

Listening. Listen for details, sequence, directions, rhyme.

Writing. Write sentences which together tell a story. Write a simple invitation or announcement.

Punctuation. Use periods after statements and abbreviations. Use question marks after questions.

Second Grade

Oral Language. Grow in clarity of expression and in conversation ability, giving and taking turns. Expand oral vocabulary.

Listening. Give attention to teaching and other presentations that are within child's understanding level. Expand in vocabulary. (People always understand more words than they use in speech.)

Writing. Understand a wider variety of writing purposes: descriptions, explanations, news stories, directions, poems, stories, plays, letters, and so forth. Grow in ability to write appropriately for these purposes. Edit own writing and find most problems needing correcting.

Punctuation. Use comma in friendly letter greetings and closings and in series within a sentence. Use apostrophe to show missing letters in contractions and to show possession.

Capitalization. Capitalize sentence beginnings, greetings in letters, proper nouns, main words of titles.

Grammar. Is introduced to the subject-predicate order of most sentences. Begin to learn about nouns, verbs, pronouns, and perhaps coordinating conjunction (and) and articles (a, an, the). Some grammars speak of "determiners" which signal nouns. These include the articles as well as possessive pronouns and other words which precede nouns (his book, that book).

Usage. Use *a* before a consonant and *an* before a vowel. Do not use double negatives. Name self last (he and I). Learn when to use lie, lay, ate, eaten, and a few other troublesome words.

Vocabulary. Understand about antonyms and synonyms, compound words, and homophones (words which sound alike, such as *their* and *there*).

Study Skills. Learn to use indexes and tables of contents. Learn to put three or four words into ABC order by the first and second letters. Learn about the children's section of the local library. Where is the fiction? The non-fiction? The easy books? Are there tapes or toys or other items besides books to check out?

Third Grade

Oral. Take part in discussions, use the telephone, show courtesy, tell things in order, describe accurately, give directions and instructions.

Listening. Understand necessary details, sequence, messages. Recognize and make rhymes.

Writing. Write good sentences and prepare book reports, stories, and friendly letters (including addressing the envelope).

Writing

Choose a good title, keep to the subject, and tell enough to make the writing interesting. Indent at the beginning of a paragraph.

Punctuation. Use periods after abbreviations and initials, and after statements, commands, and requests. Use question marks after questions. Use commas between city and state, in dates, after greeting and closing of letter.

Capitalization. Capitalize I; the first word of sentences; the first word of greetings and closings in letters; names and titles of people, names of places and other proper nouns; main words in the titles of books, poems, stories, and reports.

Grammar. Understand that a statement has two main parts— the part that names and the part that tells something about the thing named. (Complete subject and complete predicate—sometimes called noun phrase and verb phrase.)

Nouns: They name people, places, and things. Learn about singular, plural, common, proper, and possessive nouns.

Pronouns: I, you, she, he, it, we, you, and they can take the place of nouns in the subject part of sentences. Me, you, her, him, it, us, and them can take the place of nouns in the predicate part of sentences.

Verbs: There are action verbs and being verbs. Add *ed* to form past tense of many verbs. Some verbs form past tense other ways.

Adjectives: These words describe people, places, and things.

Adverbs: These words tell when, where, or how about the verb in a sentence.

Conjunction: Sometimes *and* connects two parts of a subject (Mom and I, Bob and Ben).

Usage. Use correctly: is, are, give, gave, given, did, done, saw, seen, came, come. Name self last (him and me, not me and him.)

Study Skills. Use a dictionary, finding words and their meanings, and using the guide words for greater speed. Use the library indexing system to find a book. Read simple maps.

Writing

Spelling

Spelling is automatically integrated with writing when you use the natural method of teaching writing. Thus there is no need to set up a separate subject called "spelling."

In fact, when we realize that young children are trying to learn letters and sounds and reading and writing and capitalizing and penmanship and numerous other language details besides spelling, we could decide that it is overload for many children, and spelling is the aspect that we could treat lightly while we focus on the reading and writing. Primary teachers understand that when children are required to have perfect spelling, they will write with a more impoverished vocabulary and with less creativity, so they enjoy the children's invented spelling. This shows what phonics they have learned and it shows they are trying to spell correctly.

A good time to tackle spelling hard is about fourth grade reading level when children are reading fluently and have built a good visual foundation for how words should look. In the meantime, teach bits of spelling as they fit into daily writing.

Two major school approaches are described in this chapter, and then follows the personalized approach that is much more efficient for homeschoolers. First, four principles which apply to all of spelling.

1. Good spelling is an attitude. Years of memorizing words do not add up to good spelling unless a student cares. And students who care are produced by teachers who care. Somewhere down in the list of life priorities you have to add spelling because, like it or not, the world judges our education largely on our spelling and writing. Let's hope that school officials do not receive letters that say, "I beleive that God gave parants the duty to educate there own children."

2. Good spelling includes the skill of knowing when to check on a word. A strong case can be made that this is *the* most important spelling skill, yet it is the most neglected. We get so busy with memorizing words and giving tests that we forget real life doesn't work that way. When preparing a letter, we must be able to look at it and select the words we are not certain of and check them in a dictionary or elsewhere. In the last sentence of the preceding paragraph, did you detect the three misspelled words? If you didn't, you should at least be able to detect any you are not certain of. That way you will find the three misspelled words. Train your child in this skill.

3. Good spelling begins with good pronunciation. When your child learns new words, be sure she pronounces them correctly. If she says pitcher for picture or libary for library, she will have trouble spelling these words.

4. Good spelling should be made easy. In other words, it is all right to tell a child how to spell a word instead of always sending her to the dictionary. This, again, is how we operate in real life. We avoid the dictionary if anyone around us knows the word we need. This real-life system speeds up learning, encourages the child to use a wider variety of words in her writing, and keeps her on friendlier terms with the dictionary.

Where do the words in a spelling book come from? Is there magic in these lists that will turn a second grader into a third grader? If you understand where the words come from you will decide that there is more magic in the natural method of teaching spelling and writing. There are two basic approaches used in spelling books and you can borrow something from each.

Writing

The Common-Word Approach to Spelling

Spelling researchers have listed all the words people write in daily memos, letters and other ordinary writing. They count and categorize these words and find that *the* is used six or more times for every hundred words of writing, while *and*, *of*, and *to* are used about three times each. In fact, only nine words make up twenty-five percent of the words written. Fifty common words make up fifty percent of our writing and one thousand words make up more than ninety percent.

Some spelling books, then, present weekly lists of these common words. The theory is that children should learn the words which will be most useful to them. By using the natural method of writing, you teach the same words that are in these books. That is, if the books truly do contain the words children read and write, your child will meet them in her reading and writing. And you can teach them in meaningful context rather than in artificial lists.

If you wish to check out your young pupils on the most common of the common words, here are two lists to help you.

Words which make up 25% of written language
a, and, I, of, in, that, the, to, you

Words which make up the next 25% of written language

all	from	me	this
an	had	my	very
are	has	not	was
as	have	on	we
at	he	one	were
be	her	or	which
been	his	she	will
but	if	so	with
by	is	there	would
dear	it	they	your
for			

The Phonics Approach to Spelling

Some spelling books are planned around phonics. An early list may have mat, cat, hat, and so forth. A later list may have might, fight, and right. Words are learned in groups according to phonics elements found in them.

In these books an important element is spelling rules— generalizations that apply to the use of letters, syllables, and affixes. Much controversy has arisen about which rules are really useful. If a rule has too many exceptions, is it worth teaching? Some people say No. And others say that in such a case you should just teach another rule which explains the exceptions.

Your child learns many spelling rules as she learns phonics. For instance, if a word starts with the same sound as *boy* she knows it starts with *b*. Most spelling rules fall into this category; they are so obvious that we hardly think of them as spelling rules.

Other rules are so complex or obscure that it is simpler to learn the words than the rules. For example, some systems teach that *ough* has six sounds: as in though, thought, enough, cough, through, and bough. "Rule" teachers would have children memorize the six sounds and try them in order when they meet a new word. "Word" teachers would figure that once children know a few of these words they will be able to decipher others when they meet them.

A child who learns to read by phonics already knows the consonants that have only one sound. She also knows those which have two or more sounds and which sometimes are silent. She knows the major sounds of the vowels and the sounds of most two- and three-letter combinations, such as *th*, *ck*, *ea*, and *ear*. Those basic phonics generalizations take care of spelling the majority of words.

By teaching a few additional spelling rules, you can insure that your child will be able to spell over ninety percent of words simply by phonics and spelling rules. Here are some rules with high utility.

Writing

1. *I* before *e* except after *c* or when sounding like *a* as in neighbor and weigh. This works often.

2. For *k* sound, use *k* before *e* and *i*. Use *c* before other vowels. (Cat, keg, kit, cot, cut.)

3. Change *y* to *i* and add *es*. This rhythmic rule we have all memorized works when there is a consonant before the *y*, as in baby or city.

4. Drop a silent *e* before endings which start with a vowel, but keep the silent *e* before endings which start with a consonant. Examples: baking, bakes.

5. In one-syllable words with a final, single consonant, double the consonant before an ending which begins with a vowel. Examples: running, hitting. (This and Rule 4 are how you tell that hopping comes from hop, while hoping comes from hope.) The rule also applies to longer words when the last syllable is accented. Examples: expel, expelling; but worship, worshiping.

6. Follow *q* with *u* in all common English words. In some brand names and newly coined words, this and other spelling rules are purposely violated, probably because people want to form unique words. (Examples are the double *x* in Exxon, the solitary *q* in Compaq, and the final *c* in pac.)

Personalized Spelling Approach

If the preceding sections have convinced you that spelling curriculums are not as neat as we would like, you probably will feel quite comfortable teaching your child by a personalized spelling approach. This borrows from both the traditional approaches but relies mostly on daily copying and dictation work. It branches out from there as you see a need.

When your child misspells a word, you can teach it then and there. Have her look at the model to see the difference and to correct her writing. Often that is all the help needed.

Or converse with her about why the word is spelled this way, what will help her remember it, and such. This is called "incidental teaching," which means teaching incident by incident as occasions arise. This is efficient learnng, requiring far less time than classroom style weekly spelling lists.

Other times you may notice that a particular phonics item or spelling rule may help. In such a case you can tailor a lesson or lessons to teach that.

And still other times, you may wish to fall back to the classroom list method, but individualize by gathering your own lists of words that your child needs to know. Each list should be short, just five or six words, because the child needs to learn all of them, which is seldom the case in textbook lists. A common way to use lists is to study and talk about the words, take practice tests, study more, and then on Friday take a final test. Any word missed on Friday can be carried over to the next week's list. Don't do this every week of the year, just now and then so it adds variety and change of pace to the child's language learning.

Reversing the above procedure can achieve instant learning. That is, instead of testing last, give a test first, on two or three words. Let the child see what mistakes she made, and then dictate the same words again. This is highly effective if used every once in a while on important words your child needs, but it is less effective if used too often.

In summary, personalized spelling uses these three methods.

1. On-the-spot, quick teaching in the context of a writing lesson, using mainly conversation about a word.

2. Individually tailored phonics or spelling-rule lessons.

3. Personal spelling lists

Personalized spelling is extremely efficient. Children spend study time only on words they need, not on generalized lists planned for whole classes.

Writing

In the primary grades, as explained earlier, it is best to focus on reading and writing, and let spelling take a back seat for a time to avoid overload. So the spelling ideas suggested here are to be used from time to time as seems good to you, and they should not be made into a heavy, formalized course of study separate from other language learning.

Sample Lessons

These sample lesson ideas show something of the wide range of learning levels you can meet when you use the natural method. If a child is just learning phonics, begin with one-line selections—shorter than those given here. Call attention to short vowel sounds, vowel pairs, rhymes, and so forth. If a child knows phonics and is a pretty good speller, then call attention to sentence structure, grammar, punctuation, and other such matters. And don't neglect questions which require thinking about the meaning. These sample lessons, and the method itself can be started in the primary grades, but their use should continue for years afterward. Remember that even adult writers find it an effective study method.

It is not necessary to use every idea given with these selections. You are the teacher, so pick and choose what will interest your child and profit him. Also, it is not necessary to study a selection in only one sitting. Sometimes spread a lesson over two or more days. For instance, on the first day you and your pupil may read a selection and talk about it. On the second day he could copy it, or review and write from dictation. Then he should compare and correct his copy. On the third day you could teach some grammar knowledge or thinking skill, study difficult words, and so forth, and then dictate again. When a child wants to do original writing, that takes still more time.

The goal is to help children think and learn. If that is happening, whether you race through many selections or ponder on a few, matters not at all.

If children of different ages are being tutored together they can often study the same selection. One could copy while the other writes from dictation. One could learn to spell words while the other learns grammar. One could write a shorter portion than the other. Children can dictate to each other and edit each other's papers.

These sample lessons range from Jack Sprat to quite advanced primary level. Find other selections from your home or library that are at your child's level. Use selections from any of your child's schoolbooks or from "real books." The next chapter suggests quotations from the Bible, again ranging from easy to difficult primary level.

Have the children practice neat printing for at least two years. In third grade they can begin cursive writing. Some older children do well typing or word processing their assignments.

With regular study of this kind, children gain the feel of fine writing in their bones. A bonus for you as teacher is that you will learn too. There is no end to improving command of language.

1

Jack Sprat could eat no fat.
His wife could eat no lean.
And so, between them both
They licked the platter clean.
Mother Goose

What makes these lines look like a poem? Which two lines are indented? Write all the lines from dictation or from memory. Compare yours with the model. Did you make it look like a poem? Did you spell all the words right? Which two lines have end rhymes? (The indented ones—lines two and four.) Find vowel rhymes within line one (Jack Sprat, fat). Find vowel rhymes in line three (so, both). Find out the meaning of *lean*, if you are not sure of it. If you were illustrating this rhyme, which person would you draw thin and which would you draw fat? Why?

2

One, two, three, four, five,
Once I caught a fish alive.
Six, seven, eight, nine, ten,
But I let it go again.

Mother Goose

Write from dictation, one line at a time. Did you spell all the number names right? What is the hardest number to spell? What rhymes with *five*? What rhymes with *ten*? Can you think of more rhymes for either of these? What consonants are silent in the word *caught*? Spell *caught* orally. Write it. Now write the whole poem again from dictation or from memory. Poems like this are sometimes called "nonsense rhymes." Why does that name fit? Could you think up a nonsense rhyme to help a little child learn his numbers?

3

One day a hungry fox jumped up to steal a big bunch of purple grapes. The fox jumped and jumped, but the grapes were too high. He could not reach them. At last the fox said, "I can see that those grapes are sour." This story shows that it is easy to hate what you cannot have.

Aesop's Fables

Write from dictation. Compare your copy with the model and make any corrections needed. Write again from dictation today or tomorrow. Explain why the quotation marks are used as they are. Find all the words with short *u* sound. Have you heard anyone call something "sour grapes" when they were not talking about actual grapes? Watch for the next few days to see if you or someone else makes a "sour grapes" remark.

Writing

4

Samuel looked at the first son. He was a fine and good-looking man. But the Lord said, "No, Samuel. This is not the one."

Samuel looked at seven sons. But each time the Lord said, "No, Samuel. This is not the the one."

Then Samuel asked, "Do you have another son?"

"Yes," said the father. "David is in the field keeping sheep."

When David came the Lord said, "This is the one." So Samuel poured oil on David to make him the next king.

Adapted from I Samuel 16:6-13

Does the Lord look at the outside of a person? Where does He look? See if you can find out more about the boy David. What punctuation mark follows the word *No*? Read those sentences aloud and see if you can explain why the commas are there. Explain why some of the quotation marks are there. Write from dictation, listening carefully for the comma pauses and the period stops. Try to get everything correct.

5

Henry's dog Ribsy was a plain ordinary city dog. He followed Henry and his friends to school. He kept the mailman company. He wagged his tail at the milkman, who always stopped to pet him. People liked Ribsy, and Ribsy liked people.

Ribsy by Beverly Cleary

Why is *Ribsy* capitalized? Why isn't *dog* capitalized? Why does an apostrophe and *s* follow Henry? (It shows belonging, or possession.) Write from dictation.

6

The sun was just ready to go down behind the mountains, and Heidi sat quietly on the ground, gazing at the bluebells glowing in the evening light. All the grass seemed tinted with gold, and the cliffs above began to gleam and sparkle. Suddenly Heidi jumped up.

"Peter, it's on fire! It's on fire!" she exclaimed. Oh, the beautiful fiery snow!

Adapted from *Heidi*
by Johanna Spyri

Find words that help paint a pretty picture. Find *it's* two places. The apostrophe in each stands for a missing letter. What is missing? Why do you think exclamation marks are used? Copy from the model, making sure to copy indentation and quotation marks accurately. Write from dictation.

Writing

7

Mark tore the sandwiches into chunks and held them in his hand. Ben lifted the pieces so deftly Mark scarcely felt his tongue. The bear ate them with a great smacking of lips. When it was all gone, Ben pushed at his hand, looking for more. Mark gave him the empty sack, and Ben ripped it apart, snorting and huffing at the aroma that remained.

Gentle Ben by Walt Morey

Copy this paragraph. Check your work. Who is the subject of the first sentence? Who is the subject of the third sentence? Find words that tell what Ben did (ate, ripped and others). Action words like these are called *verbs*. Find verbs that tell what Mark did. Do you think the verbs in this story help to make it interesting? Tell why or why not. Tomorrow write from dictation.

8

He was a mongoose, rather like a little cat in his fur and his tail, but quite like a weasel in his head and his habits. His eyes and the end of his restless nose were pink. He could fluff up his tail till it looked like a bottle brush, and his war cry, as he scuttled through the long grass, was: "Rikk-tikk-tikki-tikki-tchk!"

Rikki-Tkki-Tavi by Rudyard Kipling

Study the war cry to see how Rudyard Kipling spelled it. Then write this paragraph from dictation. Compare yours with the model. Be especially careful to check the commas. Could any comma be a period instead and still leave complete sentences? (Only the one after *brush.*) If Kipling had made two sentences out of this, what would be the subject of each? (He, cry.) The verb of each? (Could fluff, was.) Explain why the other sentences could not be cut in two without changing any words. A sentence that can be cut in two is called a compound sentence; it has a subject and its verb in each part.

9

The sun isn't solid, as the earth is. It is a huge, lumpy, flaming ball, made mostly of the gases hydrogen and helium. When the sun, which is a star, is compared to other stars, the sun is only medium-sized. Compared to earth, the sun is very big. More than a million earths could fit inside it.

Putting the Sun to Work by Jeanne Bendick

Put the words of the fourth sentence in a different order to make another sentence that tells the same thing. Study the commas after huge and lumpy. Can you make up a rule for using commas like this? (Put a comma after each item in a list.) Copy or write from dictation.

10

When Tom reached the schoolhouse, he strode in briskly, with the manner of one who had come with all honest speed. He hung his hat on a peg and flung himself into his seat with businesslike alacrity. The master, throned on high in his great splint-bottomed armchair, was dozing, lulled by the drowsy hum of study. The interruption roused him.

"Thomas Sawyer! Why are you late again?"

Tom Sawyer by Mark Twain

Copy the model. Tell who is speaking in the quotation. How do you know? Write the third sentence in brief form with just the simple subject and verb. Add *The* for a better sounding sentence. (The master was dozing.) Does that give you a mental image of what happened? How did Mark Twain add more to the image? Write the first two sentences also, as briefly as you can, and add the fourth sentence, which is already brief. Read the four short sentences aloud. Listen as someone else reads them. Now read Mark Twain's original paragraph aloud, or listen to it. Do you see any reason why people have loved Mark Twain's writings for so long? If you do, try to explain. Tomorrow, write the passage from dictation.

Writing

11

Do you know that the calendar is in the sky? Few people do. To know the real story behind the neat little calendars we use today, we must find out how the very ancient people made their timetables according to the stars and the moon and the sun. All sorts of mistakes were made before the ancient scientists devised a calendar system that was nearly right.

Our Calendar by Ruth Brindze

Find a word that is made of two words. This is called a

compound word. Find the shortest sentence. Find the longest sentence. In good writing, sentence length varies like this. Write from dictation.

12

After the Constitutional Convention ended, many people were not sure what had been accomplished. The story goes that a lady went up to Benjamin Franklin. "Well, doctor, what have we got," she asked, "a republic or a monarchy?"

The wise old statesman answered simply, "A republic—if you can keep it."

The Office of President
by James McCague

Find out what the Constitutional Convention was. Break these two long words into parts, called syllables. Spell each syllable. Then spell the whole words. Repeat this kind of study with other long words. What do you think Franklin meant by his answer? Ask some grownups what they think he meant. Write this from dictation. Repeat one or more times if you misspell words or make other mistakes.

13

"Uncle!" I cried. "I've got a fish."

"Not yet," said my uncle.

As he spoke there was a splash in the water, and I caught the gleam of a scared fish shooting into the middle of the stream. My hook hung empty from the line. I had lost my prize.

"Remember, boy," my uncle said, with his shrewd smile, "never brag of catching a fish until he is on dry ground."

John Greenleaf Whittier

Write from dictation without studying beforehand. Can you get the paragraphing and punctuation correct? What do you think Uncle could say next if he wanted to teach John a lesson about life? (People shouldn't brag about anything before it's done. And after it's done there is no need to brag because the action speaks for itself.) Explain why, in the last paragraph, the second part of the quotation does not start with a capital letter. If you could do better on a second try, write this from dictation again tomorrow.

14

I proposed to my brother that if he would give me, weekly, half the money he paid for my board, I would board myself. He instantly agreed to it, and I presently found that I could save half what he paid me. This was an additional fund for buying of books. But I had another advantage in it. My brother and the rest going from the printing house to their meals, I remained there alone, and, dispatching presently my light repast, I had the rest of the time till their return for study.

The Autobiography of Benjamin Franklin

What do you learn about Benjamin Franklin from this paragraph? What is the meaning of board in this paragraph? If you're not sure, ask somebody. Notice the phrase, "dispatching presently my light repast." If you were writing this, what words might you use instead? Are there other phrases you would like to change? If so, try rewriting the whole paragraph your way. Check your writing carefully. Edit and correct it until there are no mistakes. Now see if you can write Franklin's paragraph from dictation.

Writing

Bible Sentences for Writing Practice

These fifty sentences provide practice with over one hundred fifty most commonly used words. Some common words are not very simple phonetically—such as brought, sure, eyes, love. So children may not be able to sound them out, and it helps to teach such words in the context of a sentence.

Writing these sentences will do much more for children than help them learn spelling, penmanship, and sentence structure. The beauty and wisdom of Bible words will shape their minds and hearts. The majestic sound, the simplicity, the fine rhythm will develop their ears for excellent language. A child who grows into English using the Bible regularly will always be a better writer and thinker because of it. Children may use these sentences and other Bible portions of your choice from age five to age ten or more.

Beginners. First, you should make a model in neat printing for the young child to copy. If it takes him several minutes to copy "I love the Lord," you should have lessons for several days on the same sentence. After learning to copy it, the child should learn to print it from dictation as you say or spell the words for him. Next, he should learn to print it without any help in spelling, capitalizing or punctuating. Then it is time to choose a new sentence to master by the same steps. Each sentence will be easier to learn than the last.

Advanced. Older children will be able to write several sentences from dictation in one sitting. They may also check their writing against the models and learn from their mistakes.

In-Between. Between the beginners and the advanced sentence writers are the children who will profit most from this kind of practice. With these children, let them first copy a sentence or write it from slow dictation, while you give all the help with spelling and other matters that they need, so the writing is correct. In subsequent lessons, repeat the same sentence until the children can write correctly after you dictate it with proper expression.

Children at all levels may not completely understand some details, such as semicolons, but that's all right. At least they are meeting and seeing these elements at work in sentences. Later on they will understand better. That is the way of learning: some things we know well, some things we sort of know, and some things we have just been introduced to for the first time. All the learning grows together. This is why "whole" learning works so efficiently. Whole sentences, whole paragraphs, whole stories—these are the route to good writing, speaking and thinking.

In the Bible (KJV) sentences which follow, a few adjustments have been made to adapt them for language teaching. For instance, *you* is used in place of *ye*, and *makes* is used in place of *maketh*. Spelling, also, conforms to present American usage. For instance, *forever is* spelled as one word instead of two.

The sentences provide a variety of noble thoughts—praise, prayer, admonition and choice wisdom in both prose and poetry. You need not use sentences in the order presented here. And you may sometimes insert selections made by you or your pupils.

Do not have children write the references. These are included in the list in case you want to look up more information about a sentence, or if a child wants to do a creative writing assignment about one of the sentences. Also, do not use this list for memory assignments and spend a lot of time memorizing "addresses" of the verses. This language learning should focus on writing, meaning, and character building—not on addresses.

Writing

Here are ideas to use in your lessons with these sentences. They are listed in order from easy to hard.

1. Let the child either **copy** from a model or **write** from slow dictation in which you give all the help needed to get a correct copy. Use copying or dictation methods according to the child's preference. Have the child read from his copy.

2. Let the child **study** a sentence model and then write it from dictation, or from memory if he knows it. Note his mistakes, if any, and help him learn from them. Dictate again, using proper sentence expression. Have the child **read** from his copy.

3. Let the child study and write as in 2, above. Have the child **proofread** his copy to assure that it is the best he can do. Then have him **compare** with the model and find any mistakes. Dictate again, using good sentence expression. Or if the child knows it well enough, he may write from memory. Read. Compare.

4. **Dictate** a sentence the child has not seen. On the first dictation, read the sentence whole with good expression. Repeat readings may break it down into smaller parts if necessary. Compare. Dictate again.

5. Dictate a sentence whole. Repeat as needed, but always make it sound like a whole sentence. Compare the child's writing with the model. Dictate again.

6. **Review.**

7. Dictate three or four sentences, one at a time. Compare with the models. Dictate again the ones that do not match the models. This assignment is easier if the child gets to look at the models first, and harder if he does not see them first. Sometimes try it the easy way, and sometimes the harder way.

8. For an occasional **creative writing** assignment, have the child write a paragraph, story, or essay about one of the

sentences. He may tell in his own words what it means. He may tell who in the Bible said it, who it was spoken to, and what the circumstances were. He may give an example of how someone could live by the words in modern life. He may make up a story of someone living by the words today. Or he may use an idea of his own for writing. Always talk about this assignment for a time. Help the child get some ideas for writing before he has to start. If you or the pupil can't come up with some good ideas, you'd better choose another subject.

List of Bible Sentences

Easy
I love the Lord. *(Psalm 116:1)*
Love one another. *(I John 4: 7)*
Let us love one another, for love is of God. *(I John 4:7)*
Be kind one to another. *(Ephesians 4:32)*
You must be born again. *(John 3:7)*

Medium
You believe in God, believe also in me. *(John 14:1)*
But many that are first shall be last; and the last shall be first. *(Matthew 19:30)*
Your Father knows what things you have need of, before you ask him. *(Matthew 6:8)*
God has given him a name which is above every name. *(Philippians 2:9)*
The heavens are the work of your hands. *(Psalm 102:25)*
My help comes from the Lord, which made heaven and earth. *(Psalm 121:2)*
I will dwell in the house of the Lord forever. *(Psalm 23:6)*
The Lord is a great God, and a great king. *(Psalm 95:3)*
Show me your ways, 0 Lord; teach me your paths. *(Psalm 25:4)*
Ask for the old paths, where is the good way, and walk therein. *(Jeremiah 6:16)*

Writing

How much better is it to get wisdom than gold! *(Proverbs 16:16)*

A wise son hears his father's instruction. *(Proverbs 13:1)*

And you shall do that which is right and good in the sight of the
    Lord. *(Deuteronomy 6:18)*

The rich and poor meet together: the Lord is the maker of them
    all. *(Proverbs 22:2)*

And God said, Let there be light: and there was light. *(Genesis
    1:3)*

> Have you an arm like God?
> Or can you thunder with a voice like him?
>   *(Job 40:9)*

0 God, you are my God; early will I seek you. *(Psalm 63:1)*

Every man shall give as he is able. *(Deuteronomy 16:17)*

You shall truly tithe year by year. *(Deuteronomy 14:22)*

They are the eyes of the Lord, which run to and fro through the
    whole earth. *(Zechariah 4:10)*

I will take you to me for a people, and I will be to you a God.
    (Exodus 6:7)

They that seek the Lord shall not want any good thing. *(Psalm
    34:10)*

Be sure your sin will find you out. *(Numbers 32:23)*

Blessed are the pure in heart: for they shall see God. *(Matthew
    5:8)*

Little children, keep yourselves from idols. *(1 John 5:21)*

It is not good that the man should be alone. *(Genesis 2:18)*

Therefore shall a man leave his father and his mother, and shall
    cleave unto his wife. *(Genesis 2:24)*

The love of money is the root of all evil. *(1 Timothy 6:10)*

As far as the east is from the west, so far has he removed our
    sins from us. *(Psalm 103:12)*

We walked unto the house of God in company. *(Psalm 55:14)*

And whosoever was not found written in the book of life was
    cast into the lake of fire. *(Revelation 20:15)*

And whosoever will, let him take the water of life freely. *(Revelation 22:17)*

You are the light of the world. A city that is set on a hill cannot be hid. *(Matthew 5:14)*

Because I live, you shall live also. *(John 14:19)*

If a man keep my saying, he shall never taste of death. *(John 8:52)*

I am the door: by me if any man enter in, he shall be saved. *(John 10:9)*

The thought of foolishness is sin. *(Proverbs 24:9)*

And as you would that men should do to you, do you also to them likewise. *(Luke 6:31)*

Weeping may endure for a night, but joy comes in the morning. *(Psalm 30:5)*

Difficult

For there is one God, and one mediator between God and men, the man Christ Jesus. *(1 Timothy 2:5)*

And there are also many other things which Jesus did, the which, if they should be written every one, I suppose that even the world itself could not contain the books that should be written. *(John 21:25)*

You, whose name alone is Jehovah, are the most high over all the earth. *(Psalm 83:18)*

So teach us to number our days, that we may apply our hearts unto wisdom. *(Psalm 90:12)*

For if a man think himself to be something, when he is nothing, he deceives himself. *(Galatians 6:3)*

Eye has not seen, nor ear heard, neither have entered into the heart of man, the things which God has prepared for them that love him. *(I Corinthians 2:9)*

Writing

An Easy Start in *ARITHMETIC*

Contents

Arithmetic

Arithmetic Can Be Easy for Your Child

Does arithmetic have to be dull and difficult? Does it have to be frightening for you or your pupils? Must children grow up with the epidemic disease "Arithmetic Anxiety?"

The answer, as we shall show in this manual, is no.

You can make the difference. You can make arithmetic easy for your child whether you are teaching him in a homeschool or helping in his preschool years and his after school hours. In the following sections, we will examine four attitudes which are important for home educators—attitude 1) toward arithmetic, 2) toward the child, 3) toward teaching, and 4) toward testing.

1. Attitude Toward Arithmetic

Some parents, and professional teachers too, are afraid of arithmetic themselves, and thus lack confidence for teaching it. This can lead to an impersonal teaching approach and overdependence on a textbook. Just assign page 7 today and page 8 tomorrow and the child will learn arithmetic, the teacher hopes, and never discover that she doesn't understand it herself.

The cure for this brand of anxiety is to learn arithmetic yourself. You're an adult after all, and elementary school children are expected to learn arithmetic. So it can't be that hard. Get a good book and learn right along with your child. Or stay a few pages ahead.

A couple of unexpected bonuses await you after a few months of this. One is the exhilarating self-confidence that comes once you find that you don't have to go through life either hiding your arithmetic fear or apologizing for it. No longer need you excuse, "I never liked arithmetic when I was in school," or "They had that modern math and didn't teach the basics in my school." The second bonus is the joy of learning that you will experience. Your child will catch this joy from you. Your teaching in all subjects will vastly improve as you discover this heart of the teacher-pupil relationship. A teacher who loves learning earns the right and the ability to help others learn.

2. Attitude Toward Your Pupil

Some parents have a psychological or spiritual problem in relating properly to their child. One problem arises when a parent tries to live out his or her own ego through the child, perhaps pushing the child to do better in school than the parent himself did, or pushing him to do better than his neighbor's or his brother's child.

Another problem is thinking of teacher and pupil as on opposite sides of the game. A parent with this view may have had teachers who were rigid authority figures holding the answer book and the weapon of grades. If you find this tendency in your thinking, try to turn around and see teacher and pupil as on the same team. This attitude will pay off richly as you and your pupil score points together.

Some pupils learn arithmetic easily. If yours does, you can enjoy much variety, using ideas from this manual and elsewhere to give your child rich experiences in arithmetic. You may teach shortcuts, alternate methods, and almost anything you want. On the other hand, if your child has a difficult time with arithmetic, teach him one way to add and subtract. And give him lots of practice with it.

The Bible teaches us to discipline our children and to love them. These are not opposites. They blend together. Loving discipline will grow in the child into self-discipline. And that is a prerequisite for the life of learning we hope he will lead.

3. Attitude Toward Teaching

If you rate yourself reasonably high on arithmetic knowledge and on proper relationship with your child (points 1 and 2 above), then this third problem is not likely to be yours. The problem is an attitude that "they" know all kinds of things about teaching your child that you don't know.

If this problem does happen to be yours, try looking back at the decades of teaching methods and see how "science" often changes its mind. For instance, you surely have heard of stimulus-response learning even if you never signed up for Psychology 101. Just show the stimulus 2 + 3, and reward the child for responding 5. Then drill, drill, drill so the child "learns" a strong bond between 2 + 3 and 5. Don't let him think for himself because he may give a wrong answer and, horrors, he may learn an incorrect bond and you will have the job of erasing it.

That was the scientific method a few decades ago. It was developed first through the study of rats and pigeons and it dehumanized teaching methods. But it was called "science," so many teachers were hoodwinked into going along with it. The inevitable backlash followed, and in the name of science, turns and twists and fads followed one another. Science changed its mind from decade to decade. Whatever fad was on top while you were in elementary school probably influenced the way you were taught.

Can teaching and its methods really be a science in the same manner as physics and chemistry? No, it can't.

Fortunately, throughout the decades of "scientific teaching" good teachers continued to be fully human. They continued to use their intuitive common sense. They looked into children's minds as only a human can, in intense mind-to-mind contact. Such teachers led children along exciting paths of learning. Mental

Arithmetic

challenge and fun played their part—memory and drill, too. These teachers used science when they believed in it, but they used their own judgment above all.

Your child's years of growing up with arithmetic will span about one of the changing decades of teaching. Will the decade bring some "new math" not yet in view at this writing? Will it bring an earlier-is-better push because of foreign competition in business or war? Will it bring a new "scientific" method of teaching?

Whatever it brings, you can remain in control. You may read about education research, but you should digest these into your unique thinking. Your child may be an Edison who doesn't fit into an ordinary mold. Remember, no researcher knows your child as well as you do. So you can feel free to use whatever modern educators say, as long as you can digest it and live with it. But you are also free to use your own commonsense judgment. Make decisions that seem right to you.

4. Attitude Toward Testing

There is far less need for testing in homeschools than there is in classrooms. Most kinds of tests could be dispensed with until about third grade. But one kind of test will be quite useful, especially for older primaries. To help you be comfortable with decisions about testing, we include here a few comments on major kinds of tests.

Readiness tests are often given to help decide which children are "ready" for certain kinds of arithmetic work. But parents find these unnecessary because they usually know their child's abilities quite well. If there is doubt, you can simply try something and see if your pupil can do it. If it's too hard, he's not ready. Readiness tests are an attempt to manage classroom groups of children. Homeschools, at their best, should not have to imitate this testing feature of schools.

Achievement tests are those which have "norms" for comparing your child with others. Some parents, both in and out of the homeschool movement, fight achievement tests for various reasons. Some homeschoolers welcome them as a way to show the strength of homeschooling. Whatever your general attitude toward achievement tests, we recommend that you try to avoid them at first grade level, and second, too, if possible.

What if your child can do quite complex arithmetic when you pose real-life problems, but your local district wants to test him on problems written in abstract form? Professional teachers have long argued that it weakens education when we "teach to the test," and in this situation, they are right. Thus achievement tests generally don't help your child, and the pressure and misteaching which may preceed them can actually harm the child. Tests also don't help you. No arithmetic test will tell you more than you already know about your child's ability after you have been working with him for a few months. Who gains, then? The legislator, or school official, or society? Even these don't gain if your child is pressured or harmed by the testing.

So if it is within your control, try to see that your child does not meet achievement tests until at least third grade.

One test universally found in books and correspondence courses is the **unit test** appearing at the end of a unit of study. Most teaching parents feel they can skip these tests because they already know what the child can do and can't do. But correspondence schools usually require unit tests. If you are able to diminish the tyranny of this testing, especially in primary grades, it will be an improvement over the present situation. Unit tests, as other tests, help in managing large classroom groups.

But one kind of testing can be quite valuable for the child. That is **self-testing,** or testing used for motivation purposes. Use these tests after you begin formal arithmetic teaching, which will be second or third grade in most cases. Once a child can grasp

Arithmetic

the nature of the task of learning all the addition combinations, he can be motivated to study the hard ones in order to pass a test. Or he can take a test in order to see which ones he should make flashcards for. After he knows all the combinations, he can be motivated to increase his speed by taking timed tests. All such uses are part of the learning process. Teacher and pupil are on the same team. Teacher is not holding a club over the pupil.

Some unit tests can be used in this motivating way. Certain children enjoy the feel of finishing a unit and passing a test on it. Occasionally you can build a child's confidence with a unit test. "See, you *do* know it," you might say to him.

Testing decisions are many. In making decisions you are comfortable with, remember always the uniqueness of homeschools. They should not be miniature copies of classrooms.

Modes of Thinking

Children grow through three modes of thinking about arithmetic. When you understand these three modes you can easily make numerous day to day decisions about teaching. Should your child learn to recite numbers to 100 now? Does she need drill on multiplication tables or more real-life examples? You can have confidence in making these decisions.

1. The Manipulative Mode

Using this mode of thinking, children can work problems with real objects: marbles, M&M's, spoons, people. When your three-year-old helps you set the table, a lot of arithmetic thinking can happen, especially if you help it along: How many more spoons do we need? Are there enough chairs? The idea is for the child to see and manipulate real objects.

With real objects, three-year-olds can do problems that are not introduced until second grade, or later, in textbooks. Children can think about spoons, candy, fruit, and friends very early in life. And they can figure out some surprisingly complex problems. Just give them a chance.

If you happen to be familiar with Piagetian stages often mentioned in psychology books, this kind of thinking is like the "preoperational" stage. It means that arithmetic operations are not done inside the head, as we do when we multiply 5 x 8, for example. The spoons or apples are physically present and can be counted or manipulated to figure out problems.

Piagetian theory says this thinking predominates up to about ages six and seven. But it happens at all ages. Have you lately learned about computers or auto engines or anything else new?

Arithmetic

Did you get impatient with someone trying to explain and explain, feeling that if you could only get your hands on the equipment and use it then you would understand? Such an experience will help you know what the manipulative mode is.

The difference between young children and us is that we can switch freely from the manipulative mode of thinking to other modes we have learned to use. But very young children can't switch. They are tied to the manipulative mode. They must become proficient in this mode as a preparation for other modes to follow. This thinking—this actual experience with objects—is the foundation upon which all later arithmetic understandings are built.

Thus, we must teach young children in the manipulative mode. Failure to do this is probably the greatest single cause of children's arithmetic difficulties. It is why people grow up with Arithmetic Anxiety.

2. Mental Image Mode

After your child gains enough experience with spoons and other real objects, she becomes able to make images of objects in her head. She no longer needs to see and handle actual objects in order to figure out some of the easier problems you give her. Instead, she can image the objects in her head and work out problems using those images.

In the Piagetian system, this is called the concrete operational stage. This means children can do mental operations with images of objects. They can think of four family members, add one guest, and get the answer that five people will be at dinner. Or they can think of the four plates they usually put on the table and mentally add one more plate to get five.

How can you know when your child no longer needs real objects to manipulate? She, herself, will let you know by simply dispensing with their use. When she can image the objects, she finds it quicker and easier to work out a problem in her head. She becomes impatient with the slow process of counting and moving groups of checkers or plates or M&M's.

According to Piagetian theory, children use this mental image mode—along with the manipulative—until about ages twelve and thirteen. We adults find it useful, too. For example, let's say we have a story problem where we can't immediately see which number should be divided into the other to get the percentage we need. A helpful procedure is to change the numbers to small ones that we can easily image in our heads. With small numbers, our mental image tells us what the correct answer is, and we can see which number divided into the other gives that answer. After that, we translate back to the large, original numbers and work out the problem.

If you have a good feel for the mental image mode of thinking, you can be an excellent teacher of arithmetic. Children of elementary grades must do a lot of their thinking in this mode. And you will be able to communicate with them in the proper mode.

When we say that a child doesn't understand something, we usually mean that he is not able to image it in his head. The cure for that is to provide more manipulative experience. Try showing something one way and a second way and a third way. Approach it from different angles. Wait awhile and teach it again next month. After sufficient manipulative experience, the child eventually will image the troublesome process in his head. He will understand it.

3. Abstract Mode

In this mode, finally, children can think about an abstraction such as "four." They don't have to picture four plates or four dots on a domino. They have become so familiar with "fourness" that they can add and subtract this number easily. They can think

Arithmetic

of 4 x 3, where the 3 may be imaged as something quite concrete, and the four not so concrete, being the number of groups of the threes.

When do children gain the ability to think in the abstract mode? Piagetian theory puts the age at the beginning of adolescence, about twelve. In elementary school arithmetic, the abstract mode of thinking does not play a large role. You may often think abstractly yourself, but you must guard against trying to push children into this mode before they are ready. Pushing does not work. It only leads to the kinds of problems you wish to avoid: anxiety, frustration, dislike of arithmetic, and so forth.

The only route to good abstract thinking in a child's later years is through lots of manipulative and mental image thinking in early years.

How To Use the Modes

We have looked at three modes of arithmetic thinking:

1. manipulative (outside the head)
2. mental image (inside the head)
3. abstract (inside the head)

Children develop these in the order given. They can always switch back to use a previously learned mode, but they cannot jump ahead to use a mode they have not grown into. Hidden in this principle is a secret that can start you on an exciting adventure with your young pupil. Here is the secret: look at the three modes with a broad, longterm view, not with a tight, daily view.

Have you ever seen an arithmetic workbook that uses pictures to illustrate combining a group of three and a group of two, then on the same page it has problems using the symbols 3 + 2 = 5? That's two modes. And if the book tells the teacher to begin with real objects, it actually is trying to use all three modes of thinking. This is the tight, daily view. It leads through all modes of thinking in one short lesson. The next page probably takes a different set of numbers and again moves through the modes. But, of course, the young child doesn't use abstract thinking, even though he is required to use the abstract symbols.

With the broad view, you can take advantage of the young child's strengths—her manipulative and image thinking. You will spend less time with the child's weakness—abstract symbols. While thinking in her strong modes, a child can learn much more actual arithmetic. She can think more deeply, work more complex problems, and better prepare for learning and enjoying advanced arithmetic. With this broad view, you can delay teaching abstract symbols somewhat longer than is usual. Later, when you do begin to use symbols, your child will learn them faster and understand them better.

To put all this in another way, the secret is to begin the child's arithmetic at a young age by using real objects. Then spend a year or two having the child do a lot of arithmetic in her head. And after she can do that well, you finally begin working with abstract symbols. There will naturally be overlap of these three broad phases. For instance, a child may do some problems in her head while she still does most with real objects. Or she may occasionally write some problems with symbols before she is ready to use symbols all the time.

The key is that you know which mode of thinking the child does best, and you take advantage of that strong mode. This way you can teach more arithmetic. You will not waste time trying to lead up to the abstract mode each day. And you can confidently make decisions about how to use arithmetic textbooks.

A teacher once wrote, "I used to think that the fault was mine. I couldn't explain well enough, I was too impatient, I didn't motivate, and on and on. Or the fault was the child's. He didn't try hard enough. Or the family's. They didn't get him to bed on time; there was too much stress in family life. I never thought of

Arithmetic

the textbook being the problem. But then I saw that books sometimes don't fit the thinking modes of children."

You, too, can be free from slavery to a textbook. Of course, you may wish to use time-saving features a book offers. You can appreciate the ready-made problems, helpful pictures and diagrams, creative game ideas, and so on. But when you run into trouble, don't rule out the possibility that the book might not be exactly right for your particular child at that particular time.

Enjoy arithmetic. The mental challenge it offers stimulates both teacher and pupil. Sometimes it's hard work, of course. Sometimes it takes perseverance. Sometimes one must memorize. But along the way be sure to find moments of great mental exhilaration. They will come more often if you help your child use the appropriate thinking mode.

The Child's Early Years

Every day a portion of our children's conversations and problems should involve numbers and other arithmetic concepts: big, small, long, high. Comparisons. Measurements. Counting.

Three-year-old Angie counted seven people at the dinner table. "How many would be left if you and your sister go play?" Mother asked. After a moment of silent thinking, Angie answered, "Five."

Seven minus two is a problem arithmetic textbooks introduce during first or second grade. But Angie was looking at real people, not symbols on a sheet of paper. She was operating in the manipulative mode of thinking (see the preceding chapter). Her parents posed problems like this every day.

Angie gradually learned to read house numbers, page numbers, and clock numbers almost without trying. She occasionally wrote them, too. One day when she was five years old, her sister came home from school and showed her how to write a 1 in front of each number for the teens, and how to put a 2 in front of each number for the twenties. "It keeps going like that," Jill told her. Angie caught on to the pattern and spent several days filling sheets of paper with numbers. She was going on to a billion, to tentillion, she said. But one day she joined her brothers digging roads in a hillside. Roads overtook numbers as the new game in her life.

Meanwhile the first graders in Jill's class were laboriously chanting and writing numbers day after day, trying to learn them up to one hundred. A few, like Jill, had sufficient experience counting toes and counting people at dinner tables so that they understood the counting idea. They could "image" it. Thus they didn't need that much practice. Others lacked the insight Jill had, but with lots of practice they could learn by rote how to count. For both groups of children it was inefficient learning.

Not many first grade teachers operate that way today. Most realize that children must understand the meaning of numbers, and not just memorize number names. Parents could help them.

Later in this chapter are some ideas for real-life home teaching. But first, let's take a moment to see some of the many levels of teaching you might use. Consider the addition fact $3 + 2 = 5$.

Manipulative Mode	*Real objects, with touching and moving:* Three plates (spoons, marbles, jacks, etc.), put two more with them. Now there are five. *Real objects, with only sight:* Three jacks in this group, two jacks in the other group. There are five all together.
Transition Mental	*Pictures:* Picture of three jacks in a group and two in another group. Five total. *Symbolic pictures:* Three dots in this group and two in another group. Five total.
Image Mode	*Touchable objects:* Think of three jacks and two jacks. They make five all together. ("Story problems" often are of this type.) *Non-touchable ideas:* A team won three games and lost two games. They played five games all together. (Some story problems are this type.)
Symbolic Mode	*Digits only: 3* and 2 are 5. *Digits and signs: 3 + 2 = 5*

Levels for Thinking about "3 + 2 = 5"

With this chart, it is easy to see how it happens that many people make arithmetic more difficult than it needs to be. When a parent decides to teach arithmetic, what pops into his mind? Often it is the last of these modes—the symbolic. Or it may be the transitions, as found in workbooks, that pop into mind.

Unfortunately, there is a tendency to think that the manipulative mode doesn't qualify as real arithmetic. Teachers use objects to explain the meaning of symbols, or to build understanding for difficult concepts. But the goal in these strategies is to get back to the symbolic as quickly as possible. Objects are seen as only a temporary crutch.

These strategies, in one sense, are a backwards approach. If you teach a child how to read and write the digit 3 and then, with objects, teach the meaning of 3, that is backwards. That order is: 1) symbol, then 2) real objects. If a workbook lesson shows three airplanes, has the child draw lines around three toy airplanes, and then at the bottom of the page has him practice writing the digit 3, that may still be committing the same error. The order here is: 1) pictured objects, then 2) symbol. So it seems right according to the chart. But the problem is that it's all on one page. The lesson expects the child to move from manipulative mode to symbolic mode in one lesson. This kind of page should be given to a child after he already has an understanding of three. Then he may use the page to learn the digit 3. But he won't need to learn how to count three airplanes or draw a ring around three of them.

Let's examine a point further down on the chart. Children using the mental image mode (most primary children) are able to figure out many story problems by imaging them in their heads. But if they also are required to translate their thinking into symbols and write digits and signs on paper, the task is more difficult. Thus, many children who really are good thinkers in their proper modes are made to feel like failures.

Arithmetic

This chart and the accompanying discussion is given here to remind us adults of the complexity of thinking skills we acquired during our growing up years. Symbolic thinking doesn't happen overnight. We need to give our children time. We need to be patient with them. We should not start arithmetic teaching with 3 + 2 = _____ .

Real-Life Arithmetic

Parents teaching their children at home have an exciting opportunity. Future progress in education can happen more in the homes than in schools. One reason is that parents can use real-life situations for teaching. Another reason is that parents have the advantage of using the child's early years. As more parents become interested in teaching, society is likely to develop a new attitude toward these early years. No longer will we want to put children in classrooms earlier and earlier. Home is the best environment.

If you are homeschooling, you are pioneering in a highly significant movement. Don't throw away your opportunity by imitating school too closely. Use real life for teaching. Your family is unique and will have other kinds of situations than are listed in this manual. But all families can follow two important principles, no matter what the specific activities are.

The first principle is to use real-life situations to teach bits of arithmetic and to build a "need" to know arithmetic. When you read stories to children, they learn that books contain stories and they develop a "need" to learn how to read stories for themselves. That same principle must apply in arithmetic. Daily events involve arithmetic. Share these with your child so he develops an awareness of arithmetic and a need to know it.

The second principle is to do this sharing in the mode appropriate for your child's age and development. At preschool ages, that will practically always be the manipulative mode. At primary ages the manipulative will gradually give way to the mental image mode. Occasionally, your child may wish to read and write numbers. That is all right. Just don't push him to work problems written in symbols. Most arithmetic should be mental. It happens in conversation, not in written assignments.

The following list gives some of the places these conversations can occur.

Game Area. Is this your family room, kitchen table, or living room rug? Wherever it's located, you must have this. We list the game area first, so you will read it even if you don't take time to read the rest of the list. We cannot overemphasize the importance of games for growing children. Much arithmetic is learned as children count moves, compute scores, take turns. But that is only a fraction of the benefits. Numerous thinking skills are developed as children learn to operate within various kinds of rules, plan strategy, and so forth. Sportsmanship and other social skills gradually develop. When children later learn that rules don't have to be rigid, they can develop new twists and live by their own agreed-on rules. One fifth grader developed an insurance system to accompany Monopoly. He calculated the chances of a player landing on Park Place with a hotel on it, and other expensive events, and balanced this against money he could collect as players pass Go. Then he sold insurance against expensive contingencies. Players could purchase various kinds of policies and make installment payments each time they passed Go. This is complex for young children, of course, but the point to notice here is that years of game experience lead to advanced thinking skills and creativity.

Supermarket. Young toddlers sitting in the basket can watch as you put in *one* loaf of bread, *two* cartons of milk, and so forth. Older children can help select *six* apples. Still older children can carry pocket calculators and figure out that the chocolate

Arithmetic

Santas, even at half price, cost more per ounce than other chocolate in the store.

Kitchen. Young toddlers can find you a "bigger" pan and a stirring spoon with a "longer" handle. Slightly older children can help you measure and count to follow a recipe. They can begin reading ingredient lists. Children don't have to be very old to follow some simple recipes entirely on their own. Making milk drinks, fruit drinks, sandwich fillings, and other snacks will teach them to read both the words and the numbers in a recipe. Learning about measuring cups and spoons, quarts, ounces, pounds, and such kitchen matters comes to children bit by bit through regular experience in using them. You don't need to get preachy. Just have fun making the cookies.

Dining Area. Setting the table, arranging chairs, and such preparations are ideal for counting and adding experiences. Sometimes subtraction and multiplication are needed too. Later, when the family is eating, arithmetic can be one of the topics. Does anyone have game scores to report? Simple money matters to discuss? Did you walk *two* miles instead of your usual *one?* If arithmetic doesn't accidentally come up, you can invent problems, such as Angie's mother had a habit of doing.

Yard, Garage, and Workshop. Chores carried on in these areas all have their natural arithmetic. Measuring, counting, planting rows. Here is where families show their uniqueness more than in the kitchen. One father had his seven-year-old son help with carpentry work almost daily. The boy learned many skills along with arithmetic. Another father let his son help fix the motorcycle. He learned about bolt and wrench sizes and other mechanical matters. What kind of arithmetic experiences does your home offer?

Car. Speed limits, miles to the next town, street numbers, license numbers—the list is endless. Don't feel that your child needs to completely understand these concepts as you talk about them or read them from signs. This is a time for him to meet them over and over and gradually develop meaning. Older children can read road maps and compute mileage. Younger children can count three cows or find the tallest building. There's something for everyone.

Television. If you have this in your home, let your child learn more than what's on the screen. He can learn to tell the times of his favorite programs. He can plan for the number of viewing hours per day or per week that you allow him. He can read channel numbers and program listings.

Real life is daily. It is close at hand. It offers the best learning opportunities your child will ever have. Think arithmetic!

Arithmetic

First Grade

Arithmetic goals are not the same everywhere. Textbooks and school curriculum guides vary in what they suggest teaching in each grade. Thus there can be no one "right" curriculum plan for you to follow. This chapter gives guidelines which are "typical" of most first grade courses, and you should feel free to use them somewhat flexibly. If you don't get it all taught this year, don't panic. Just plan to teach it next year. A more likely situation is that you will find your child well ahead of these guidelines, particularly if you have done a thorough job of real-life, manipulative mode teaching.

The first section below gives you a scope and sequence chart. It shows the knowledge and skills typically taught at first grade level. The second section adds comments and teaching suggestions especially for homeschools.

First Grade Knowledge and Skills

Numbers. Count cardinal numbers to 100. Ordinal numbers (first in order, second, third, etc.) up to "tenth." Child must understand and use numbers, not simply chant their names. He should be able to count out fifteen sheets of paper, point to the fourth person in line, count beads, and so forth. Some experience in reading numbers and a little experience in writing numbers may be offered if the child seems ready for writing in general.

Groups. Ability to see how many are in a group such as dots on dominoes. Ability to count by groups of five and ten, using materials such as an abacus or nickels and dimes. Ability to count by twos, using pairs—eggs in a carton, eyes and ears of the people present, socks in the wash, and so forth.

Measurement. Gain simple practical experience with clocks (both dial and digital), calendars, rulers, measuring cups and other measuring devices. Use money—at least pennies, nickels, and dimes.

Vocabulary. Grow in ability to use words having to do with size, quantity, shape, and other arithmetic and geometry concepts. Examples: taller, larger, less, circle, square, one-half, hour, minute.

Addition. Ability to add any two groups with sums of six or less, not including zero as a group. Some children may proceed to problems with sums up to ten. (Refer to the addition chart in the second grade section.)

Subtraction. Ability to "take away" a group from six (or ten) or any lesser number and tell what is left. (Other kinds of subtraction problems, such as finding how much more are in one group than another, are not used when children first learn to subtract.)

Notation. Ability to read and perhaps to write the digits from 1 to 10. If addition and subtraction problems are written out, begin with the "sentence" form, thus: 4 and 2 are 6.

First Grade Teaching Suggestions

Practically every item in the first grade curriculum can be taught using real-life methods. In fact, they are better taught in real life, including games, than in daily sit-down arithmetic lessons. Let the child spend real money at the store. Let him help make cookies. Read again the previous chapter, and use those ideas, extending them to fit your child's growing understanding.

As a homeschool teacher you do not need a workbook and daily written assignments such as a classroom teacher might use.

Arithmetic

Your one-on-one teaching can accomplish more. But if your child likes it, occasional use of a workbook is all right. If you are using a correspondence course which requires daily written work, see if you can reduce the writing and have the child do some of the problems mentally or with objects. Also, you may look into local law. It may be the case that your child doesn't have to be enrolled in anything until age seven or eight.

If you feel bold enough to strike out on your own without a workbook or mail-order course, be sure to plan regular check-ups for yourself. Reread the scope and sequence several times during the year. Mark it up. What does your child know quite well? What weak area will you give special attention to? Plan a game or activity and some arithmetic conversations for each day. (See the activity list below if you want help in getting started.) At this level it is not important in which order you teach the topics. Just be sure the child keeps meeting arithmetic.

If you feel more secure following a textbook, a good compromise is to look at the book yourself but have the child do much of the work in his head or with objects.

Don't be deceived by the short list of first grade topics and by how simple they look to us adults. For a child of first grade age, it takes a considerable amount of learning to master the knowledge and skills listed for this grade.

Notation. This last item on the list is, surprisingly, less important than any of the others. The others involve genuine arithmetic thinking and learning. This item involves only a skill in writing things the way our society has decided they should be written. If a child labors too hard at this task, you can safely wait until his physical development allows for easier small muscle movements.

Measurement. This should only be learned through practical, real-life experiences. No attempt need be made to work problems. The emphasis is on learning the principles of measurement, which are: 1) Any measurement, such as an inch or hour, is always the same no matter what ruler or clock it is on. 2) To measure correctly requires practice in being exact. 3) Two people measuring the same object should get the same results. Repeated use of simple measurements builds an understanding of these principles.

A ruler with inches only, no fractions, is helpful. These can be bought at educational supply stores. Teach inches, not fractional parts thereof. Teach time only to hours, not halves and fourths. Teach anything that comes up in everyday life—*pound* of butter, *cup* of sugar, *gallon* of milk.

Activity Ideas. This list is given to show how easy it is to achieve arithmetic learning in the daily activities around your home.

Domino-type games (matching, recognizing groups)

Lotto-type games (reading numbers)

Board games (counting moves, following rules, reading numbers)

Jacks (counting, recognizing groups)

Pick-up-sticks-type games (counting, scoring)

Building toys—Lego, blocks, and others (size, pattern, comparison, planning, counting)

Snacks (counting, sharing equally, cutting in half)

Follow simple recipe (reading numbers, measuring)

Help fix things (accuracy, conversation, measuring, comparing)

Help with shopping (money, counting, comparing)

Follow directions for an art or craft project (straight lines, folding in half, following steps 1, 2, 3, etc.)

Collect rocks, stamps, other (sorting, comparing, classifying)

Arithmetic

Second Grade

Every second grade teacher meets a problem each fall that no other teacher faces to the same degree. The problem is the forgetting that occurs over the summer between first and second grades. It is wise to begin each topic by going over first grade work. Review adding and subtracting. Reteach measurements. Play number games. Ease back into arithmetic. This time will not be wasted. It will pay off in faster progress as you move ahead to new understandings.

Thus, in the second grade topics listed below, you will see the first grade curriculum included in each. If the child learned numbers to 100 in first grade, we do not say that second grade curriculum covers the numbers 101 to 200 or higher. But we say that second grade curriculum covers all the numbers to 200. This is standard procedure, and many years of experience have proven to second grade teachers that it is necessary and that it works well.

As suggested in the first grade section, you may teach most of the knowledge and skills without expensive workbooks. Your second grader may enjoy a little book work. But use books in addition to real life teaching, not instead of it.

Second Grade Knowledge and Skills

Numbers. Read, write, and count up to at least 200. Ordinal numbers up to "tenth." If a child understands calendars well enough, she may learn ordinal numbers up to "thirty-first."

Place Value. Understand the tens and ones places in numbers up to at least 39. This is simply an introduction to the place value idea; the concept will be taught again in third grade. (See teaching suggestions below.)

Groups. Ability to count by tens and fives at least to 30, and on to 100 if the child can. Ability to count by twos to 10 or higher. (Use real objects—stacks of books, checkers, popsickle sticks, squares on a game board. Use dimes, nickels, and pennies after a child understands the value of these coins.)

Measurement. Time in hours and half hours; length in inches and feet (no fractions); coins of pennies, nickels, dimes and perhaps, also, quarters and half dollars; and a few other simple measures such as pound, pint, quart, and dozen.

Vocabulary and Signs. Learn the words *subtract* and *minus* to use instead of *take away.* Learn *plus*, *add*, and *equals.* Extend vocabulary of comparison: long, longer, longest; high, higher, highest; left and right; top and bottom; and so forth.

Fractions. One-half, one-fourth, and sometimes one-third. By cutting apples or candy bars, the child learns these fractional parts. No work on writing fractions is done. No adding or subtracting of fractions. And no fractions with numerators other than 1.

Addition. Ability to add two numbers up to sums of 12. Ability to add three numbers. For children who understand place value and who write problems in their vertical form, you may begin addition of two-place numbers without carrying.

Subtraction. Ability to take away a group from twelve or any lesser number and tell what is left. With the same prerequisites mentioned for addition, you may teach subtraction of two-place numbers without borrowing. (See teaching suggestions for further comments on this.)

Multiplication and Division. Begin to understand the meaning of combining similar groups two "times" or three "times."

Arithmetic

Begin to understand the meaning of dividing a large group into smaller groups of twos or threes or fives or tens. (Work with real objects rather than with problems written in abstract form.)

Notation. Learn to write addition and subtraction problems in both their horizontal "sentence" forms and their vertical forms, using and knowing the signs. Examples:

$$4 + 2 = 6 \qquad \begin{array}{r} 4 \\ +2 \\ \hline 6 \end{array} \qquad 6 - 2 = 4 \qquad \begin{array}{r} 6 \\ -2 \\ \hline 4 \end{array}$$

Two-place numbers in addition and subtraction and columns of three numbers in addition may be added to these notation skills for children who are proficient in working the problems. (See teaching suggestions below for a discussion of early notation versus delayed notation teaching.)

Problem Solving. Much experience in solving problems is usually given in second grade. This will not be new or difficult for children brought up from an early age in real-life arithmetic. Continue to use the manipulative and mental image modes of thinking. Occasionally write problems in their abstract forms.

Second Grade Teaching Suggestions

Place Value. Perhaps the most difficult concept you will have to teach is that of place value. This is helping your child to understand why digits 1 and 4 occupy the places they do in the number 14. Fourteen is a good first lesson on place value because it sounds almost like four-ten. Eleven, twelve, and thirteen are words invented by someone other than a primary teacher.

To teach place value manipulatively, you need some kind of objects which can be easily bundled into groups of ten. Popsickle sticks are often used. You could have the child count fourteen sticks and notice that it's a rather slow way to find out how many sticks there are. Would she like a faster way to count them? Have her count ten sticks and bundle them together with a rubber band. Put the group of ten at the left and four single sticks beside it at the right. How many? Was that faster than counting each one singly? Put six single sticks at the right of the ten. How many? Continue playing with the sticks in this manner, sometimes letting the child make problems for you to count.

When this is easy to do with one bundle of ten, proceed to two tens and three tens. When you can't stump your pupil on any number up to 39, proceed to writing the numbers. Lay out fourteen sticks and directly below them show how we write 1 to tell that there is one "ten" and we write 4 to tell that there are four "ones." Practice other numbers, giving your pupil turns at being "teacher."

Repeat some of the same procedures using dimes and pennies. Repeat using an abacus or other teaching aids you happen to have. Sometimes use the mental image mode. For example, while driving in the car you may ask, "How would you show the number 26 with the sticks?" Answer: two bundles of ten and six single sticks.

This technique of teaching a concept several times in several ways is a secret of good teachers everywhere. You will find it useful for any subject your child finds difficult.

Abstract Notation. Understanding this item is the key to choosing your strategy for the early years of arithmetic teaching. The question is: Should you teach abstract notation as early as the child can learn it, or should you use the time, instead, to teach in greater depth in the mental image mode?

Abstract notation includes writing out a column of numbers to add, and writing one number under another before subtracting it. The digits and signs used are "symbols." The position of the numbers is an arbitrary decision of society. They are conventions

Arithmetic

that adult, abstract thinkers use as a kind of shorthand to speed up our thinking.

When we teach these to children, we must realize that we simply are introducing them to our abstract "tools." We are not suddenly turning children into abstract thinkers. And the danger of starting too early and pushing this kind of work is that we will spend an inordinate amount of time with it. We will be teaching the importance of making straight columns, writing numbers in certain places and other trivial matters. By calling them trivial, we don't mean that they are unnecessary. But they are small matters compared to real arithmetic thinking.

If you stay with meaningful mental arithmetic longer, you will find that your child, if she is average, can do problems much more advanced than the level listed for her grade. You will find that she likes arithmetic more. And when she does get to abstractions, she will understand them better. She will not need two or three years of work in primary grades to learn how to write out something like a subtraction problem with two-digit numbers. She can learn that in a few moments time, if you just wait until she is pretty good at mental image subtraction.

Mental Image Mode. While delaying abstract work, do plenty of real-life arithmetic. Use games a lot. These don't have to be "educational" arithmetic games, since most popular children's games require arithmetic thinking. If your child can do it, begin some experiences with the hundred chart described in the third grade teaching suggestions.

Addition and Subtraction Chart. The following chart shows in a concise way what your teaching task is in addition and subtraction. You can be flexible, of course, in order to meet the needs of your particular pupil. But this chart will help you know the general grade levels for teaching the various facts.

For addition, the chart reads like an old-fashioned

multiplication table. That is, you choose a number in the left column and a number in the top row, and the sum of these is found in the chart where the row and the column meet.

For subtraction, the procedure is reversed. Start with a number within the chart, subtract the number at the beginning of its row, and the answer is the number at the top of its column.

The dark lines mark off the grade levels. Most first graders learn everything down to the line below the sixes, and many continue to the line below the tens. Most second graders learn up to the twelves. And third graders learn the whole chart.

	1	2	3	4	5	6	7	8	9
1	2	3	4	5	6	7	8	9	10
2	3	4	5	6	7	8	9	10	11
3	4	5	6	7	8	9	10	11	12
4	5	6	7	8	9	10	11	12	13
5	6	7	8	9	10	11	12	13	14
6	7	8	9	10	11	12	13	14	15
7	8	9	10	11	12	13	14	15	16
8	9	10	11	12	13	14	15	16	17
9	10	11	12	13	14	15	16	17	18

ADDITION AND SUBTRACTION CHART
Grade 1: to sixes or to tens.
Grade 2: to twelves.
Grade 3: to eighteen.

Activity and Game Ideas. The following list of activities shows how everyday items can be used for arithmetic. Regular use of such activities achieves the "life application" that school teachers are always striving for. As a home teacher, you have an

Arithmetic

advantage. Life application is all around you.

Learn to make phone calls to Grandma, to a friend. Prepare a list of emergency numbers and post them in a convenient place.

Try to read some household bills. Talk about how to save money.

Read advertisements and cents-off coupons. Talk about them. Would this really save us money? Do we need the item, or would we just be letting the advertiser talk us into spending money? Is this brand with its cents-off coupon a better buy than some other brand?

Make up problems about news stories. If the team had made one more touchdown, what would the score be? Were there fewer traffic deaths this year or last year?

Read the calendar, the thermometer, the speedometer, the scales.

Read all the numbers in headlines on the front page of the newspaper.

Use commercial games a lot. They help to develop many arithmetic, logic, and thinking skills. Here are a couple of homemade games to add to your game collection.

Secret Number

For two players. Each has twenty nickels (or other coin). Player A writes a secret number from 1 to 100. Player B guesses and pays one nickel for the guess. Player A points upward if the secret number is higher than the guess, and she points downward if it is lower. Player B continues guessing and paying until he guesses correctly. Then he writes a secret number and Player A pays him to guess.

If one player runs out of money, the other is the winner. If neither player runs out of money, they can stop after an even number of turns and count to see who has the most money.

Variations. For easier games adjust the range of numbers. For instance, guess numbers from 1 to 10, and use only five coins.

The Greatest Number

For two or three players. Each player needs a set of ten cards, with the digits from 0 to 9. Players each mix up their cards and put them in a pile face-down in front of themselves.

To begin, all players draw three cards and make the greatest number they can with them. The player with the greatest number wins a point. Mix the cards again and take another turn. The player with the most points by the end of a specified time period is the winner.

Variations. For practice in writing numbers, you may draw and show the cards, and your pupil is to write the largest number she can with them. If you can make a larger number, you win. If you cannot make a larger number, she wins.

Draw two cards or four cards to make the game easier or harder.

Third Grade

At about third grade age, pupils can profit from more sit-down, formal arithmetic lessons. They may write their computations more often than before, and they may work in more systematic fashion toward mastering arithmetic skills. Now is the time to consolidate the real-life learning of previous years.

During this time of consolidation, point out often to your child what he knows and what he is now learning. Say things like, "I remember when you couldn't add big numbers like 7 and 8. Now you can add practically anything." Without such help from you, your pupil is not likely to be aware of his progress. You can see progress, since adult minds can take a sweeping view above the ground. But young children are down among the blades of grass. They can't see well where they have been and where they are going. Your frequent reminders can help keep your pupil motivated.

At third grade, you may feel a need for using a textbook for the first time. If you do use one, remember to continue teaching the meaning of arithmetic operations. Don't depend too heavily on pages in a book to do all the teaching for you. And feel free to skip parts in a book that your child is already proficient with. A common situation is that a book may teach what pennies, nickels, and dimes are, while the child may have extensive experience handling these coins in real situations. In cases like this, don't feel guilty passing over the pages, or letting the child do them simply "for fun," if he wishes to. You are teaching the child, not the book.

Third Grade Knowledge and Skills

Numbers. Read, write, count, and use numbers up to at least 1000.

Place Value. Review ones and tens places. Extend to the hundreds place. Notice the use of zero in a number like 106.

Groups. Expand skills in counting by groups. Become proficient in counting by tens and fives up to 30 or higher. Count by twos up to 20. Try counting by threes and fours. Sometimes begin the counting at numbers besides zero.

Addition and Subtraction. Master all facts in the addition and subtraction chart. (See chart in the second grade section.) Games, flashcards, speed tests, and other drill devices should be used to achieve ease and speed in using these facts. Learn carrying, borrowing, checking, and bridging (adding across the decades, as from the twenties to the thirties).

Multiplication and Division. Understand the principles that multiplication is a way to add equal groups and division is a way to subtract equal groups. Learn multiplication tables of twos and threes first. Tens and fives may follow if pupils have sufficient background in counting by these groups. Ones may be added when pupils understand the rather odd concept of one "times" something. All together, about half of the 81 multiplication facts should be taught. (See teaching suggestions below.)

You may introduce the multiplying of two-digit numbers which do not require carrying. This may involve more attention to zeros than has been given heretofore.

Fractions. Extend understanding of fractional parts of a real object, using only 1 as a numerator: one-half, one-fourth, one-third, one-fifth. Learn to write a few fractions which have 1 as a numerator. For some children, fractional parts of groups may be introduced. For instance, one-half of twelve or one-half of four

Arithmetic

may be learned using real eggs, candy, or other objects.

Measurements. Ability to work with all coins and with dollar bills. Write amounts, using decimal points and dollar signs. Compute problems involving money (within the guidelines given above for addition, subtraction, multiplication, and division). Build understanding of hours, half hours, and quarter hours. Learn about days, weeks, months, and years. Use the measures of inches, feet, and yards, and convert from one to another. Use pints, quarts, gallons, ounces, and pounds in realistic situations. Read scales and thermometers.

Problem Solving. Continued and expanded experience in solving realistic problems is the most valuable part of third grade arithmetic. Use problems involving games, sports, and other topics of high interest to your child. Solve many of these mentally or on the hundred chart or number line. Solve some by writing the figures in their proper positions.

Teaching Suggestions for Third Grade

Subtraction with Borrowing. The word *borrowing* has been used for centuries. But teachers have long pointed out that nothing is returned, as we usually do when we borrow items. If your child has a good understanding of place value, if he has bundled sticks into groups of tens and hundreds, then you may wish to use the term "regrouping." For instance, in the problem below, a ten is mentally moved to the ones place. Thus the top number is regrouped as 3 tens and 13 ones. Then the subtraction can proceed.

$$\begin{array}{r} 43 \\ -\ 6 \\ \hline 37 \end{array}$$

Multiplication. A multiplication table which goes as high as 9 x 9 includes 81 multiplication "facts." Third grade curriculums generally teach about half of these facts. But they do not all teach the same half. The facts you teach will depend on the approach you wish to take. One approach is to teach by "tables." That is, you may teach the table of twos up to 2 x 6 or 2 x 9. Then follow that with the tables of threes, fives, tens, and perhaps ones.

Another approach is to teach by "families." A full family includes two multiplication facts and two division facts, thus:

$$\begin{array}{cc} 6 \\ \underline{\times 2} \\ 12 \end{array} \qquad \begin{array}{cc} 2 \\ \underline{\times 6} \\ 12 \end{array} \qquad 6\overline{)12} \qquad 2\overline{)12}$$

Since you probably will use both approaches at different times, it may become a bit confusing to keep track of which facts your pupil knows. Besides, when you are consistent in teaching the meaning behind arithmetic facts and operations, the child can figure out facts which you have not specifically taught him.

For these reasons, we do not show on a chart the exact facts to teach. But if your child knows about 40 of the easier facts, he has done well. He may not know 7 x 8, but he should know 3 x 5.

Fractions. Third grade curriculums ordinarily do not include adding or other computations with fractions. Instead, children should continue to gain real-life experience and build meaning for the difficult concept of fractions. Cut fruit into halves or fourths. Cut candy bars into thirds. See how many ways the child can cut a sheet of paper into halves.

To teach how fractions are written, you may show the meaning this way:

$$\frac{1 \text{ of the}}{4 \text{ equal parts}} \quad \text{is shortened to} \quad \frac{1}{4}$$

Textbooks. If you are using a workbook or textbook of some kind, learn to see it as a guide through the many topics of arithmetic. Realize that the child need not work every problem on

Arithmetic

every page. As mentioned earlier, it sometimes is appropriate to skip pages. Often it is best to talk through a problem with the pupil. Let him try to image it in his head, or if he cannot do this, let him work it manipulatively with objects. Teaching in this manner, you will not cover as many problems each day, but your pupil will learn more from the problems he does work.

Teaching Aids. Two extremely valuable teaching aids are a hundred chart and a number line. These have so many uses that it is worthwhile to make one or both of these. A hundred chart is included in this book. You or your pupil may wish to make a sturdier version of it. To make a number line, number from 1 to 100 in one long row. Use a strip of adding machine paper, tape a strip of masking tape along a wall, or whatever creative way you can manage this in your house. A string of 100 wooden beads could also be used—ten yellow, ten blue, ten yellow, ten blue, and so on.

These teaching aids can help children to visualize numerous aspects of arithmetic operations. See the list of suggested primary grade uses on the last page of this manual.

Game Ideas. At third grade level, you should continue to use commercial games and other standard games and puzzles. These develop skills in thinking, planning, strategy, logic, and arithmetic processes. As your child grows in ability he may become the family scorekeeper, to add more arithmetic even to word games. Here we provide you with a few game and activity ideas specifically for use during arithmetic class periods.

A Problem a Day

Each day either you or your child can make up a problem from some piece of paper that comes into your family life. Possibilities are: menu, cash register tape, airline or bus schedule, newspaper bill, grocery ad.

Zap

For two or more players. One player begins counting with 1, the next says 2, and so on. But for 5 and all multiples of 5 players must say "Zap." When this is easy, try Zap for multiples of 3 and of other numbers.

Concentration

Make eight pairs of cards with addition or multiplication facts your child needs to learn. Put a problem on one card and its answer on another. Example: 8 + 9 on a card and 17 on another. Mix the cards and lay them face down in random positions or in rows.

The first player turns over two cards. If they match he keeps them. If they do not, he turns them down again. The second player then takes his turn. When all pairs are matched, the one with the most cards is the winner. Later, add a rule that each player must name the match he is looking for before turning over a second card.

Invent a Game

Use old game boards, spinners, markers, and other game parts. The pupil is to think up a new use for the board. He may make cards or any new parts he needs for his game. For a language assignment, he can write the rules. Rules should tell: 1) how to prepare, 2) how each player takes a turn, and 3) how to determine the winner.

Advanced Skill Drill

Write numbers from 0 to 99 on cards. Mix them and place them face down. The pupil selects two cards and subtracts the smaller number from the larger. If the subtraction is too difficult for him to do on paper, let him work it on the hundred chart or with objects such as popsickle sticks. For addition practice, write numbers to 50. (This activity is especially helpful for people teaching without textbooks. A day's allotment of problems can be determined in this way.)

Arithmetic

Exactly Twenty

For two players. Prepare forty-five cards by printing 1 on five cards, 2 on five cards, and so on up to the number 9. Mix the cards and place them face down in a pile. To begin, each player draws two cards.

The object of the game is to collect cards which total exactly 20. The first player starts his collection by laying one of his cards face-up in front of him. He then draws another card. The second player does the same. Turns continue. When either card in a player's hand would make his collection total more than 20, he cannot add to his collection, but must use his turn to discard and draw a new card. The discard pile is face-up beside the main pile. The first player to collect exactly 20 is the winner.

Ways to Use the Hundred Chart

The hundred chart on the pull-out poster is one of the most flexible and useful devices you will ever find for helping your child to understand numbers and the basic arithmetic processes. Use it almost every day in your teaching. The list of ideas below will help you get started. (Most of these activities may be done on a number line, as well.)

Easy

Count to 10. Count to 20. Count as high as you want.

What is 5 and 1 more? Three and 2 more? (Count forward for any simple addition problem.)

What is 1 less than 6? One less than 8? Two less than 5? (Count backward for any simple "take-away" subtraction problem.)

Advanced

Count by tens on the chart. Count by fives. By twos.

Count by tens, but start on the 3, or 6. Start on other numbers.

Count by any size group you can. Start anywhere you wish.

Add 5 to 7. Add 5 to 17. To 27. To 37. (This bridges from one row, or one decade, to the next.)

Add 3 to 9. Add 3 to 19. To 29. To 39.

Add 9 to any number. (Nine is especially fascinating because of its position as one less than 10. Later on, 11 can be fascinating in a similar way.)

Write a rule for adding 9 to any number. For adding 11.

Write rules for other discoveries you make on the chart.

Make up addition problems with bridging. Can you bridge all rows?

Begin with 100 and count by tens backwards. Count by fives or twos backwards.

Begin with 20 and count by twos backwards.

Subtract 4 from 51. Subtract 4 from 41. From 31. From 21. From 11.

Subtract 5 from 53. From 43. From 33. From 23. From 13.

Make up subtraction problems with bridging. Can you do them them on all the rows?

When you have a difficult problem to figure out, see if you can work it on the hundred chart.